OTHER TITLES OF INTEREST FROM ST. LUCIE PRESS

The New
LEADER

Bringing Creativity
and
Innovation to the Workplace

The New
LEADER

Bringing Creativity
and
Innovation to the Workplace

Gregory P. Smith

St. Lucie Press
Delray Beach, Florida

Phone: (407) 274-9906
Fax: (407) 274-9927

S^t_L

Published by
St. Lucie Press
100 E. Linton Blvd., Suite 403B
Delray Beach, FL 33483

This book is dedicated to the memory of the two most influential people in my life. My father, William Edward Smith and my Scoutmaster, John Winterowd.

Also to my best friends, and my family: Cathy, Heather, Hannah and Garry

TABLE OF CONTENTS

PREFACE

At no time since the Industrial Revolution has the world faced so many challenges and also so many opportunities. The power of technology today staggers what was available just a few short years ago. But even with its sophistication, speed, and capacity, the greatest of the world's resource remains untapped. The mind with its imagination, conceptual thinking power, and creative and innovative ability remains the greatest of the world's resources.

Each day people rise out of bed, get dressed, and journey to a place where they conduct an activity—commonly called work. Commuters in Washington DC, travel along the beltway headed toward Capital Hill. In Atlanta, they board the Marta and head toward Peachtree Street. Not far from Stuttgart, Germany, in the town of Nelligan, workers get on the S-Bahn heading to the Mercedes plant. In Puerto Rico, students zip along the twists and turns of the calles toward the Ponce School of Medicine.

No matter the location, no matter the industry, our life centers around a work routine. Whether we work at home, or in the traditional office or factory, this pattern repeats itself day-in and day-out.

Businesses face revolutionary changes. The changing and increasingly more competitive world has created a need for new ways of doing things. Even a successful past is no guarantee for success in the future. We can no longer do the same things the same way and expect job security and a comfortable and successful lifestyle. Starting today, as we enter the doorway to the future, let us ask ourselves several questions. What can I do to make this time more productive and rewarding? How can we overcome bureaucratic rules and regulations and capture the potential of the workforce? Is this job going to exist two years from today? Are we doing the right things?

Many organizations resemble hippos—unattractive, unresponsive, and bureaucratic places to work. Margaret Wheatley talks about how many organizations have become like fortresses with secret passageways where those with special keys can pass through. The driving forces in the world today are people and their ideas, not control and authority. We can no longer merely afford to manage people, but we need to learn how to manage ideas.

The Challenge Today

The work environment today is under assault. Company loyalty, trust, and motivation are under the attacks of a changing economy. Both fear and uncertainty plague many people's minds, a chaotic work environment.

A recent issue of *Human Resource Executive* magazine outlined major challenges facing human resource executives: (1) how to manage change, (2) how to improve quality, and (3) how to increase productivity. These challenges are not only unique to human resource executives, but to all leaders and managers in the business world.

We must rethink the entire concept of the word "work." Much of the difficulty lies in how we structure our organizations and how we treat people in these jobs. Structure, rank, titles, and position on the organizational charts and those initials at the end of the name sometimes get more value than the latent potential in all of us. Good people get trapped in a bad system, therefore inhibiting creativity and innovation. What separates the winners and losers is leadership. Good leadership creates an environment where everyone feels as if they are part of the organization and allows them to contribute to the enterprise.

Why I Wrote this Book

I spent a career in a variety of leadership positions working with people in and outside the United States. During my career, I was an Army officer, maintenance supervisor, hospital administrator, dental manager, Executive Officer for a Mobile Army Surgical Hospital (MASH), faculty member, and a management consultant.

My experience in the military showed me the amazing accomplishments of what good people will do when they are properly lead and believe what they do is important. As a management consultant, I have worked with many organizations, ranging from car rental agencies, banks, healthcare, facilities, federal and country governments, school administrations, telecommunications companies, the military, and others.

This experience has shown me that there is a commonality we all share. All people, no matter their level in the organization, education, or background, want to do a good job—they want to be exceptional.

Our greatest resource is the ideas of and the diversity of our people. There are over 140 languages spoken within our borders, and hundreds of faiths and religions practiced by people of all colors. This diversity represents new and important ways of doing things. This is our strength, not our weakness. This isn't just a book about diversity. It is a book about managing ideas and how these ideas can make our organizations more competitive, productive, invigorating, profitable, and efficient.

New Leadership

All this requires a new style of leadership. Leadership is the golden thread holding all these separate threads together in a cohesive fabric. A leader is a person who inspires you to take a journey to a destination you wouldn't go to by yourself. The new leader is a person who creates an innovative environment that unleashes the natural creativity and the potential of the workforce.

Whether we realize it or not, all of us today are leaders. Effective leadership is not complex, nor does it require a degree from a university. As leaders, we all can make a tremendous difference.

The new leader removes barriers and obstacles built up over years of bureaucratic management. The barriers and obstacles may be bureaucratic rules and restrictions, or perceptual barriers of rank, title, and position. This new leader provides direction and looks out for the needs of people. This person helps to create an environment of pride and loyalty, not fear and intimidation. When reading this book, you will notice several important themes:

Key Themes:

- We need to rediscover the chemistry between organizational performance, people, and their ideas.

- The "idea" is the universal motivator, the most powerful force in the world.

- How can we make management theory really work?

- How can we make a bureaucracy innovative and creative?

- Why "work" must add meaning to life.

- The key role of leaders and how they can make a difference.

- We must face change or face extinction.

- People are more important than the system.

Peter Pan

I live an exciting life and get to travel often. However, despite my enjoyment for work and travel, I hate to leave my family. Before leaving on one trip, I piled my three children into my car, and we drove around town. The idea came to me to use the car as a way to spend some "quality time." I thought a good way to begin was to ask that famous question parents ask their children the world over. "What do you guys want to do when you grow up," I said. Little did I know at the time how their answers would change my thinking about work and life.

My oldest daughter began, and she said, "Daddy, when I grow up I want to be a veterinarian." Well, I thought that was logical and rational. You see if you knew my oldest daughter, you would have known that she will make the perfect veterinarian. Her life centers on rescuing various animals and creatures from harm's way. At that particular time in her life, she had an iguana, a dog, a Siamese cat, a collection of frogs, and toads. She even once brought home a snake. I said to myself, "Yes, that is rational and logical. She would be a good veterinarian."

Without dropping a beat, my middle daughter proudly began. "Daddy, I want to be a school teacher." Yes, that was rational and logical. My middle daughter would make a good school teacher. If you knew my middle daughter, you could see her taking my 5-year-old son, sitting him in front of a black board with ruler in hand, teaching him the rules and precepts about how to be a perfect little brother. "Yes, that is rational and logical, she would be a good school teacher," I thought.

Now, what would my son say? Would his goal for his life proudly follow in my footsteps? Would he want to be like me?

The Journey

My 5-year-old son sat quietly thinking for a few moments. Then his dream unfolded to our shocking amazement. Excitedly he said, "Daddy, I want to be Peter Pan, I want to fly!"

"What! , want to fly!" I stopped myself short, thinking, "That is not rational and that's not even logical!" But then it hit me how wrong I was. Well, why can't we fly.? Then I recalled a memory from my past. I remembered those days when I wanted to fly, too. As a child I put a towel around my shoulders and jumped off the living room couch. Then I grew up and for some reason the dream faded away. Why?

Often we let the system steal our dreams, smash our goals. How many times have we heard, "You can't do that here." "That idea won't fly." "Be an astronaut? Your grades aren't good enough!"

America is blessed with the greatest natural resources. These natural resources are the people and their ideas. No nation is as fortunate as we. As leaders, we must make work more than a job. Work should be a place where we can use our imagination, use our creative energy, bring enthusiasm, and take flight. This is what *The New Leader* is about.

This book is not the be all and end all of organizational performance. It is a work in progress, like "The Never Ending Story." I invite all of you to become part of the journey by sharing your ideas, tips, advice, and success stories. At the end of this book is a New Leader Registration Form. Feel free to tear it out and mail it to us and share your ideas. This way you will become a living and vital part of this journey.

I can be reached at:

Chart Your Course International
2814 Hwy 212, SW
Conyers, GA 30208
Phone: (770) 860-9464
Fax: (770) 760-0581
E-mail: 74344.135@compuserve.com

ACKNOWLEDGMENTS

The result of a book is never a singular effort. This book is no exception and is the result of many contributions from many people and in many different ways. I particularly want to thank Susan Houdek for her many contributions, editing, and support. Her encouragement and dedication became a valuable part of this book.

In San Antonio, thanks to Linda Arnold, Rich DeMouy, and Hilda Shepeard for several years of friendship, support, and management practice. In Atlanta, many thanks to Eddie Duke, Brenda Scales, and Paula Davis for allowing me the privelege to work with you. We should all be proud that we made life that much better for many people. Thanks to all my newspaper editors who allowed "Bottom-Line Business" to become a printed reality.

To all the others who made this book a living reality: Phillip Williams, who placed the spark in my mind many years ago; and Garry and Gloria, my wonderful in-laws who showed me what hard work, loyalty, and dedication is really all about. Thanks to Drew Gierman of St. Lucie Press, who gave me the chance and the opportunity to write this book.

Special thanks to:

★ Mel Crissey for being a wonderful mentor.

★ Joe Moffatt for your exceptional leadership.

★ LTG A. J. Guy LaBoa for the opportunity to serve with you and to see a leader who really cares.

★ Bruce Nelson, the editor of the *Army Medical Department Journal* for your insight and editing ability.

★ Harry Noyes, who provided me some great material and insightful discussions.

★ Mitch Ditkoff, President of Idea Champions, for enlightening conversations.

★ Celome Miller at the Veterans Administration Medical Center in Portland, Oregon.

★ To all those National Speakers Association friends who gave me advice, support, and assistance. I particularly want to thank George Morrisey, Dianna Booher, Bob and Jane Handly, Naomi Karten, Terry Paulson, Scott and Melanie Gross, David Byrd, Kay Baker, and Jill Griffin.

★ To John Posey, a real inspiration who showed me how to stay young and keep dreaming.

★ To Darci Kitchens, who made thousands of copies for me at Office Depot in Conyers, Georgia. Her work is remarkable and truly appreciated.

★ To Sandy Koskoff, my production editor, and to Sandy Pearlman, my project manager at St. Lucie Press, for all their help.

★ Thanks to Harvey Siegel-Williams, an ex-Marine and a man of many artistic talents.

★ To my mother, Tina, who gave me the gift of curiosity and showed me that we all can make a difference.

Finally, to the United States Army for a wonderful career, the privilege of becoming a leader, and the opportunity to be all I could be. To all those Non-Commissioned Officers who kept me on the ground and in the right direction.

CHAPTER 1

CAPTURING THE INNOVATIVE SPIRIT

"To win, we need to find ways to capture the creative and innovative spirit of the American worker. That's the real organizational challenge."
—Paul Allaire, CEO, Xerox

The satellite spun just out of reach of the astronauts. Two rescue attempts failed, and the space mission was taking a turn for the worse. Pierre Thuot, Thomas Akers, and Richard Hieb floated near the shuttle payload bay realizing they faced a serious dilemma.

In May of 1992, the Space Shuttle Endeavour blasted from its launch pad at Cape Canaveral. Its mission was to recover the Intelsat VI satellite 22,400 miles above the earth. The satellite had fallen from its planned orbit, and years of research and millions of dollars hung in the balance.

What was supposed to be a routine space mission had suddenly taken a turn for the worse and had become a potentially dangerous situation. Any mistake at this point could result in personal injury or the loss of the $70 million satellite.

The highly trained crew of the Endeavor was specifically selected to handle the complexities of this recovery mission. Inside the shuttle was a special Recovery System Arm designed to delicately

1

grab the huge satellite and gently tuck it into the payload bay. With two attempts behind them, the astronauts scrambled to find new ideas on how to precede with its capture.

With the hands of a surgeon, mission commander Dan Brandenstein aligned the Endeavour within a few feet of the satellite. This would be the final attempt to capture the satellite. They were running out of time, and they needed a solution quickly. This was their last chance.

Orders were relayed from NASA to halt the mission. Both scientists and NASA experts were trying to determine the best solution. A brigade of computers and scientific calculators figured trajectories and approach patterns. As the minutes clicked by, the shuttle crew waited for advice and directions on how to precede. Back on Earth, millions of Americans sat mesmerized in front of their television sets watching with awe and fascination. Then something totally unexpected happened.

The development unfolded in front of astonished NASA officials at the Johnson Space Center. Hundreds of innovative ideas poured into the Johnson Space Center from across the country. Americans were writing, calling, and faxing the Space Center. Fax paper covered the floor. Phones were ringing off the hook. School teachers, school children, plumbers, business people—representatives from all walks of humanity contributed their ideas.

There were many ideas. Each ingenuous idea was unique and different. Some of the ideas consisted of various techniques using ropes, hoops, nets, duct tape, and combinations of other resourceful devices. Some ideas were carefully drawn out by engineers. Others were colored by school children with crayons. Each innovative idea represented someone's initiative and their natural problem-solving ability. Each person hoped his or her idea would solve this galactic problem, including the one shown on the next page.

One idea in particular stood out from the others in its creativity. The person suggested that one astronaut should clothe himself in a Velcro space suit and have another astronaut tie a rope around his waist. Then the strongest astronaut could throw him onto the spinning satellite. Once attached, they could reel the satellite and the attached astronaut back into the payload bay!

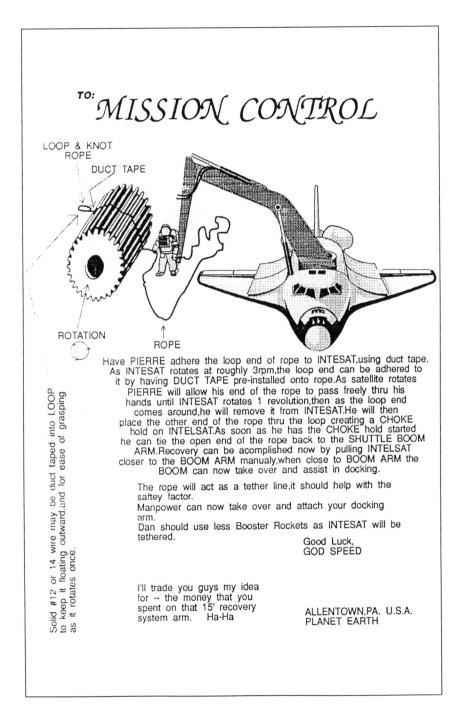

TO: *MISSION CONTROL*

LOOP & KNOT
ROPE

DUCT TAPE

ROTATION

↑
ROPE

Solid #12 or 14 wire may be duct taped into LOOP
to keep it floating outward,and for ease of grasping
as it rotates once.

Have PIERRE adhere the loop end of rope to INTESAT,using duct tape.
As INTESAT rotates at roughly 3rpm,the loop end can be adhered to
it by having DUCT TAPE pre-installed onto rope.As satellite rotates
PIERRE will allow his end of the rope to pass freely thru his
hands until INTESAT rotates 1 revolution,then as the loop end
comes around,he will remove it from INTESAT.He will then
place the other end of the rope thru the loop creating a CHOKE
hold on INTELSAT.As soon as he has the CHOKE hold started
he can tie the open end of the rope back to the SHUTTLE BOOM
ARM.Recovery can be acomplished now by pulling INTELSAT
closer to the BOOM ARM manualy,when close to BOOM ARM the
BOOM can now take over and assist in docking.

The rope will act as a tether line,it should help with the
saftey factor.
Manpower can now take over and attach your docking
arm.
Dan should use less Booster Rockets as INTESAT will be
tethered.

Good Luck,
GOD SPEED

I'll trade you guys my idea
for -- the money that you
spent on that 15' recovery
system arm.   Ha-Ha

ALLENTOWN,PA. U.S.A.
PLANET EARTH

Finally, back at NASA, they reached a consensus and made the official decision. The third attempt successfully captured the satellite. It was safely stowed in the space shuttle, and the astronauts and crew returned to a hero's welcome back on Earth. The American public cheered and celebrated the victory. Interest in the space program was revitalized. Outer space was conquered—human over machine—a tribute to American ingenuity.

In the process, NASA and the astronauts had not only captured the satellite but also the imagination of the American people. To me, the most fascinating aspect of the mission was something entirely different, something tremendously more significant. I was fascinated by the innovative spirit of the people represented with each of the proposed solutions submitted. This space mission did not just demonstrate ingenuity, but it illustrated a principle about people. NASA created an environment that unleashed human potential—the problem-solving power of people. To this day, only a few people appreciated the true significance of what really happened.

Secret of Success: The Innovative Power of Ideas

Throughout history, stories like this repeat themselves. People rise against tremendous odds, overcoming personal hardships. Businesses on the brink of financial failure are rescued and regenerated by a determined leader. A crisis sparks a high level of performance which returns to normal after the event is over. New businesses spring up and ride the wave of new technology while capturing market share.

Are these stories and situations anomalies, or is there a pattern? Think about it—if ordinary people can provide practical solutions to the capture of a runaway satellite in outer space, just think what they can do back here on Earth. What is more important, could businesses and organizations use this energy and vitality to make organizations more efficient and productive? I think so. The outcome is a dynamic vitality, a vitality that can tear down any obstacle, any barrier, and knows no bounds.

Innovation Meets Bureaucracy—Walls Falling Down

In November of 1989, the Berlin Wall and the border between East and West Germany came down. I visited the border a few years before its destruction. I vividly remember the event. It was a gray and rainy day. We were escorted to within only a few yards of the border. The gray bunkers and towers stood above row after row of barbed wire, mine fields, and guard dog runs on their side of the fence. Armed guards watched us through binoculars.

The Wall stood for decades representing everything wrong with Communism. The border stood in the way of freedom, creativity, and the human spirit. Today, the Berlin Wall stands no more, but in its place is a new barrier to freedom—a wall of bureaucracy. The wall of bureaucracy is found all around the world. It is found in almost all organizations, governments, churches, schools, and businesses.

Many businesses have rules, regulations, and policy manuals that look more like a set of encyclopedias. Excessive policies and procedures are like sacks of bricks tied around workers' necks. Nordstroms, a very successful department store, has an employee policy manual consisting of only one rule—"Use your best judgment." Nordstroms realizes that with fewer restrictions, workers empower themselves to be more pleasing to the store's customers. Leaders must initiate a conquest seeking to destroy bureaucratic procedures and tear down obstacles hindering innovation.

Like the Berlin Wall, bureaucracy and old leadership styles form barriers and obstacles restricting human freedom and creativity. Eventually, if it goes unchecked, bureaucracy becomes overly restrictive and rigid, creating unproductive work environments.

The Berlin Wall did not collapse because of a new weapon, new technology, or political posturing. People yearning for freedom tore the wall down. People today want to be the best, but barriers and obstacles within a system won't let them—the system gets in the way. Too much bureaucracy saps their potential, creativity, and natural problem-solving ability. What is important to realize is that bureaucracy goes beyond just red tape and paperwork.

Bureaucracy limits the way people think and the way they behave, holding them prisoners.

A bureaucratic environment saps the innovative and creative potential of people. Ideas and the creative ability of people can become like innovative lightning bolts. The collective force of these bolts of lighting start forming small cracks, then the cracks grow into larger fractures until finally, they break through. When innovation meets bureaucracy, the walls come tumbling down.

Tremendous Potential

Paul Allaire, the CEO of Xerox, said, "To win, we need to find ways to capture the creative and innovative spirit of the American worker." Within all of us there is an immense reservoir of potential waiting to be tapped. Often this potential lays dormant until the right person, the right conditions, or a new form of leadership can bring it to life.

Around the country I am beginning to see a new optimism in people and with the many opportunities available before us. This outlook is probably different than what you see and hear around the country. For the moment, let's put the headlines aside and look at the big picture.

The United States still remains the most powerful nation in the world. We are the most powerful nation for many reasons. Understand that "powerful," in this case, doesn't necessarily mean military might, a balanced budget, or a Congress that works amiably together. If you haven't realized it yet, the "seat" of power isn't in Washington, DC. Frankly, it doesn't really matter what happens in Washington. The seat of power rests with the people. True power is recognized in the ideas, dreams, creativity, and ingenuity of America's people. This is real power, and it is why we stand head and shoulders above all other countries in the world.

America is still the land of opportunities and of dreams. The difference between those who can see opportunity and those who only see problems is one of personal choice. We as individuals choose between mediocrity and opportunity. I always remember what Zig Ziglar once said about why foreign-born American citizens seem to achieve financial wealth quicker and easier than American-born citizens. He said that when they come into this country, they are wide-eyed and overwhelmed by all the opportunities available to them. They work so hard and are so industrious by the time they realize America has problems, they are already rich.

Our greatest resource is the ideas of and the diversity of our people. There are over 140 languages spoken within our borders, and hundreds of faiths and religions are practiced among people of all colors. Those languages and skin colors represent new and diverse ways of doing things. This is our strength, not our weakness. To capture this potential is our greatest challenge.

Each morning when we get up, we choose between a good day or a bad day. We choose to get upset at the fool tailgating our car. We decide whether or not our boss will get us upset. We allow others to make us a victim or victor. The choice is in our hands.

Walt Disney was a great visionary leader. In his mind materialized the innovative concepts and ideas of Mickey Mouse, Disney World, Epcot Center and all of his other creations. Even with his imaginative power, he knew he was limited. He knew he needed something else.

Walt Disney
"You can dream, create, design and build the most wonderful place in the world...but it requires people to make the dream come to a reality."

America stands on the threshold of an exciting world full of opportunities. We have every right to be optimistic about the future. Today, people in the United States enjoy more freedoms and more rights than ever before. We of all nations have the ability to make a difference and to improve the world. You as an individual have the ability to make a difference—don't ever forget that.

Guiding Principles

Until I wrote this book, I often wondered what were the special ingredients that transformed people and businesses from ordinary to extraordinary levels of performance. Repeatedly, my research and experience have shown me that there are conditions which lead to higher levels of innovative performance. I have turned these conditions into the following guiding principles.

→ Work must form a bond between life and the human spirit.

→ Work should be a place where people can reach their ultimate potential.

→ Work must add value and have meaning; therefore, people are more productive when they understand how their work fits in the big picture.

→ Counterbalance information technology with meeting the interpersonal needs of workers.

→ All people, no matter what their background, culture, or level of education, want to do an excellent job and want to be successful.

→ People will achieve amazing accomplishments when they believe their contributions are important and will be used.

→ Top management is responsible for creating an innovative environment of leadership by providing direction, removing obstacles, and building trust.

The Innovative Environment: The Framework for Success

This is a leadership book that shows how to redesign and energize businesses by using a three-step framework. The framework shows you how to channel workers' creative energy and ideas toward the goals of the business.

The successful business of the future will be one that provides unequaled customer service, delivers an exceptional product or service, and continuously makes innovative improvements. Success in the next decade will depend on managers and leaders capturing the innovative hearts and minds of their workers. This will only happen if businesses breathe, dream, and allow innovation at all levels of the business. Preoccupation with gimmicks, short-term thinking, and bureaucratic rules and procedures will generate more "Going Out of Business" signs than anything else. Innovation comes from a workforce empowered by both their ideas and their ability to contribute to the enterprise.

Creating this innovative environment is the greatest business challenge of the 90s and beyond. Innovation begins with the leader or business manager. In today's rapidly changing work world, the manager must be more like a coach or a team leader than a boss, a collaborator instead of a manipulator. The leader must create an environment which supports and nurtures innovation. We are seeing a new world where passion rather than knowledge, where chaos rather than structure, are the norms.

Today, citizens and customers hold the government and all organizations to higher standards. People want solutions to crime, tax inequities, and the declining infrastructure. The old style of management is obsolete, unproductive. We must tear down the walls of bureaucracy replacing them with innovative ways of managing. The stories throughout this book, combined with my own experiences, show how people are capable of tremendous accomplishments. Like climbing a steep mountain, the challenge is difficult, but the rewards are tremendous.

How do you become an innovative business leader? You must AIM for it. The three keys in the innovation framework are *Access,*

Information, and *Motivation.* As shown in the following graphic, there are three components, or three characteristics, which lead to an innovative environment. Each one is explained below.

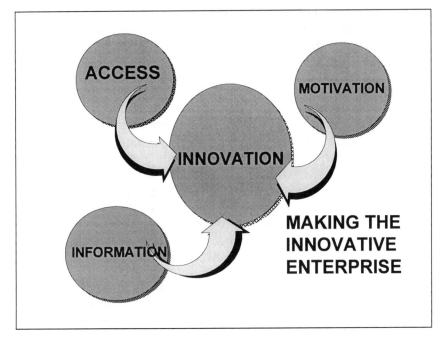

Accessibility

The first part of the innovation framework is accessibility. The major organizational challenge facing us is to make everyone, particularly workers, active participants in the work process. The innovative enterprise ensures that everyone is accessible to each other at all levels within the organization. Accessibility to each other facilitates a feeling of teamwork, trust, and equality. This not only includes workers, but customers and suppliers as well.

Most organizations are infected by both visible and subtle barriers—limitations based on rank, position, and structure. Hierarchical chains of commands, rank, and titles affect workers' access to each other. These subtle barriers are like unwritten rules of conduct. They determine who can talk to whom. Organizations make it clear, often unconsciously, that top management's role is to think and the workers at the bottom of the hierarchy are to carry out the orders and dictums of those above them. Access by everyone to everyone fosters creativity, helps the flow of innovative ideas, and speeds up the decision-making process.

A major factor that encourages accessibility to each other is the organizational vision. The vision connects personal goals and dreams of workers with the goals and objectives of the business. Vision statements point describe the direction in which the organization is heading. This unifies everyone's efforts toward a common purpose.

Information

The new leader must not only be concerned with the management of people, but with the management of information. The environment is constantly changing and poses a major challenge for individuals, businesses, and organizations. In times of change, people within the organization need more information, and it has to be communicated more effectively.

The innovative enterprise must constantly adapt, create, and innovate. Information and communication comprise the wind that sails the innovative enterprise toward its destination. Yet, information and communication pose difficult challenges for most businesses. The difficulty lies in balancing the flow of information between providing too much or too little information. Managers complain that they are overloaded, while front-line workers complain that "no one tells them what's going on!"

In the traditional organization, information represents power. The flow of information is important to keep the enterprise on course. Those businesses faced with a rigid hierarchy have a limited flow of information. They have real difficulty staying current and flexible. They end up pushing instead of leading their organization to the next juncture. On the other hand, the innovative enterprise effectively uses information and communication to keep everyone informed and able to work together.

Businesses must concern themselves with providing the right information at the right time in the most effective manner possible.

The right kind of information is called *"innoinformation."* This type of information is critical to the vitality of the enterprise. *Innoinformation* consists of the plans, vision, goals, and all the new ideas affecting the enterprise. The innovative enterprise is looking forward, continuously changing and adapting to the needs of the customer. By providing *innoinformation*, everyone in the enterprise can see new opportunities, not just the people at the top. Idea campaigns, teamwork, benchmarking, and other programs keep the organization flexible and vital.

One way to ensure people are ready to change is by communicating the ideas and suggestions made by the people within the organization. A constant flow of ideas and suggestions show people that there is a need for change. When people hear new ideas, they are more willing to change. They become more adaptable and flexible, thus removing the biggest hindrance managers face in traditional organizations.

Jack Jackson, a professional speaker from Ft. Worth, Texas, said, "If you are going to innovate, you must communicate or you won't motivate!" His words prepare us for the third and final component of the innovation framework.

Motivation

Motivation is a complex process critical to any organization's success. It is important to understand that people become more innovative when motivated. As life becomes more complex, so do the needs and expectations of the people who work within our businesses. What motivates one person may not motivate another. However, there are several common threads running through the motivational fabric of the innovative enterprise.

People who feel they are contributing to the organization are more motivated. Employment is more than hiring a pair of hands, and people today want to feel they are contributing to the business. Personal recognition remains as one of the most important elements leading to high motivation. People rewarded for using their brains add a tremendous energy boost to the company. Providing pats on the back, ice cream parties, and other simple celebrations create a feeling of pride that makes everyone a winner.

One of those common threads leading to higher motivation is creating a pleasant working environment. Barry and Eliot Tatelman are entrepreneurs who created a work culture around having fun. These two brothers own Jordan Furniture, which is located in Massachusetts. Everything from their zany television commercials, purple painted parking lots, and their Multimedia Motion Odyssey Movie ride, commonly known as MOM, helped them to build a million-dollar industry. Their "raving fan" concept attracts shoppers filling their 700-space parking lot.

They built the fun culture by surprising their employees. Once they played the *William Tell Overture*, and both Barry and Eliot rode into the store on horses dressed as the Lone Ranger and Tonto. Their fun behavior stimulates their employees to go out of their way to creatively help customers.

Loading dock employees occasionally dress in tuxedos. When shoppers drive around the back to pick up their furniture, they surprise them by washing their car windows, car tires and provide free hot dogs. There are no high pressure sales people selling stuff no one wants.

American Ingenuity

Few people are as ingenious as the American soldier. There was no exception to this during Operation Desert Storm. Give a soldier a roll of duct tape ("1000 mile-an-hour" tape) and look out. Consider the solder who fashioned the portable toilet. Stored on the back of a Humvee was the innovative toilet seat heading across the desert. It was a steel gray folding chair with a hole cut out in the seat. Mounted on the seat, with olive drab "1000 mile-an-hour tape," was a styrofoam swimmer's ring. An innovative solution to a perplexing problem.

Several years ago the world's attention focused on an 18-month-old toddler who fell into a dry water well in Midland, Texas, somehow becoming trapped deep underground. It seemed an impossible predicament. People from around the world volunteered to aid in her rescue. Ideas varied from a man with no collarbones who could squeeze himself down the shaft, to the idea of sending trained TV monkeys down to pull her up. Other ideas included sending a weather balloon down to Baby Jessica. Then the balloon could be inflated with helium bringing Jessica up with it. Another woman suggested dropping tennis balls down so

Innovative companies invest in human resource programs, employee development, and continuing education. Low innovation companies end up spending much more money hiring replacements due to high turnover and low morale.

Jessica could work her way up. Finally, someone wanted to attach a sponge soaked in glue to a string, stick it to her head and when it was dry, start pulling.

Early arriving soldiers during Operation Desert Storm discovered that entertainment and recreation equipment was hard to find. To make up for what they could not find, they made their own. One group created their own weight-lifting equipment by using cinder blocks and water jugs. The jugs were filled with sand and a little water. Finally, the entire apparatus was completed by taping it to camouflage poles. Baseball was another activity subject to soldiers' ingenuity. A mattock handle and a ball of tape went a long way before the real baseball equipment arrived.

A group of innovative workers won a $77.1 million Lotto jackpot in Austin, Texas. Every time the Lotto hit $40 million, the front-office workers at the Win-Holt Equipment Company formed a pool. The workers developed a special system for selecting lotto tickets and a method of splitting the winnings. Finally, five workers who had the lucky numbers split the winnings.

CHAPTER 2

REINVENTING HOW WE WORK

"To succeed in this world, you have to change all the time."
—Sam Walton

Winston Churchill once said, "There is nothing wrong with change as long as it is in the right direction." Today's changing business environment resembles a roller coaster more than anything else. Zig-zagging market conditions, changing consumer demands, and skyrocketing technological advances are giving business managers nonstop headaches. Managers face perplexing problems on how to stay competitive, including reducing cycle time and keeping the workforce trained on the latest skills, techniques, and processes. Now, more than ever, it is important to know what you are good at in order to reinvent, redesign, and position yourself in the right direction.

The Changing Work Environment

Intellectual capital has become the number one resource to business success. Since the trend to downsize started in the mid-80s, businesses have faced difficult realities. Fewer and fewer organizations can afford to work by trial and error anymore. Businesses' adaptation to change must be immediate, flexible, and, if possible, proactive. Those who don't adapt will find themselves in serious trouble.

The saying, "do it right the first time," is more true now than ever before. Here are some specific changes that have taken place in many companies, perhaps even in yours.

→ Key management positions and training people, people with the most experience, have been displaced.

→ A culturally diverse workforce has emerged, demanding special skills and abilities from management.

→ A skilled labor shortage has developed. Companies are picking up the slack and are having to provide basic education to people entering the workforce.

→ Managers are unfamiliar with how to manage teams, improve quality, and increase productivity.

→ The marketplace is more competitive, changes occur more rapidly, and mistakes are much costlier.

→ The body of knowledge and required skill levels necessary to be successful is growing exponentially.

→ Customers, citizens, and employees expect more from those who lead them.

→ A litigenous environment has emerged.

Businesses today must find new ways to motivate, revitalize, and transform the workforce. Here are other factors influencing the workforce today.

Lost Customer Focus

The Sears Tower rises majestically out of downtown Chicago. In sad contrast to its appearance, this tower draws attention to everything that went wrong with Sears Roebuck & Company. For decades,

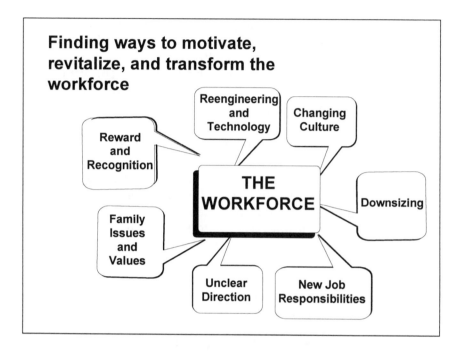

Finding ways to motivate, revitalize, and transform the workforce

Reward and Recognition

Reengineering and Technology

Changing Culture

THE WORKFORCE

Downsizing

Family Issues and Values

Unclear Direction

New Job Responsibilities

Sears dominated the retail store industry. Sears *was* the retail store industry.

In the 1960s and 1970s, few could come close to matching the might of Sears and Roebuck. There was a Sears store in almost every mall in America. They grew larger and larger, becoming more diversified. They expanded from strictly a retail department store business to an array of services, including insurance, home repair, investments, etc.

Research shows that as the company grew in size, there was less need for leadership. A "caretaker" mentality started taking over. In fact, there was a time when Sears had five CEOs serve an average of 3 3/4 years each. It usually takes that long just to figure out what is wrong and make a change.

Merchandise prices inched up higher, and it became more difficult to find a salesperson available to operate the cash registers. Warehouses overflowed with Sears merchandise waiting for someone to buy it. During these years, Sears failed to react to changing consumer trends. Competitors were coming up the back stretch at full throttle. When Sears finally woke up in 1992, the red ink represented a loss of $3.9 billion. Wal-Mart, Sam's, K-Mart and others helped rob Sears of it's glory and tradition. The venerable "Christmas Toy Catalog" became a casualty to cost cutting and remains part of a proud history, probably never to return.

The Journey Along the Highway of the Future

The highway of business success is littered with organizational road-kills. Businesses face two impediments along the highway toward the future. Those two impediments are success and bureaucracy. No longer can businesses maintain status quo and expect to remain competitive. Those businesses continuing to do the same things the same way will find themselves out of business, replaced by new industries and customer sensitive competitors. Because of this rapidly changing and chaotic business world, there is new meaning to the word "insanity."

INSANITY: TRYING TO DO THE SAME THINGS, THE SAME WAY AND EXPECTING A CHANGE.

Success is always a dangerous milestone for any organization. Businesses in trouble today are not there because they have made serious mistakes. They are in trouble because they have failed to adapt and change. What made them successful yesterday could be what makes them unsuccessful tomorrow. Rapid growth, expansion, and huge profits causes many companies to make serious errors, get lazy, and fall asleep. These errors can later become fatal when economic conditions or consumer tastes change. This is particularly true when a competitor can do something cheaper and better. Consider the following changes in technology:

OLD	NEW
Carbon paper	Copier machine
Phono record	Compact disc
Sailing ship	Steam ship
Water power	Nuclear power

Bow and arrow	Guided missile
Flint and steel	Butane lighter
Telegraph	Cellular phone
Hot air balloon	Space shuttle
Typewriter	Word processor
Postal/telephone service	Internet
Sears Toy Catalog	Penney's Toy Catalog

Success leads to a predictable cycle of events. Peter Drucker said, "Whom the gods want to destroy, they will send 40 years of success." Past success is always an enemy of the future. Sears' successful past blocked it from seeing the reality of the future. This was clearly displayed when the Wal-Mart's and other huge warehouse stores started moving into towns and cities across the United States. The U.S. military experienced a remarkable victory during WW II, only to send an unprepared and under-equipped expeditionary force to fight in North Korea.

Success causes another dilemma—with people. The same people who led the organization to success in the past could be the very same ones who are now roadblocks toward future change. Leaders must ask themselves two questions. Are we looking toward the future or are we languishing in the past?

The journey to the future is guarded by a thousand people appointed to protect the past.

Change happens faster and faster. Computer and software companies come and go in an ever-changing working world. Computer microprocessors become obsolete every 6–8 weeks. This changing environment is what caused Andrew S. Grove, Chairman of Intel, to say, "There is at least one point in the history of any company when you have to change dramatically to rise to the next performance level. Miss the moment, and you start to decline." There are several other reasons organizations face trouble today.

→ Failure to meet customer needs and expectations.

→ Failure to involve the worker in the work process.

→ Management by structure and rigidity.

→ Missing leadership, a "caretaker" style of management used instead.

→ Failure to focus on the work process.

→ Development of a slow and complex decision-making process.

→ Inability to identify and correct mistakes.

→ Failure to adapt and change quickly.

The second impediment toward the future is bureaucracy. Bureaucracy slowly builds up like fatty deposits along arterial walls. Too much fat paralyzes organizations, locking them into old patterns and habits.

A bureaucratic organization creates two groups of people—those who make the decisions, and those who carry out those decisions. The decision makers have the power and authority. The decision makers become isolated from day to day reality, not seeing what is happening in and around their organization. They end up spending more time solving yesterday's problems while everyone else is sitting on their hands waiting for a decision to roll downhill. Finally, once decisions are made, they are selectively passed down like manna from heaven for the rest of the people to act upon. This type of organization becomes slow, inflexible, and has low levels of innovation.

Bureaucratic organizations have many talented and dedicated people. They want to do a good job. They want to be committed, but the system forces them to wait, to sit on their hands, frustrated, and powerless to make anything happen. After a while, even the most dedicated workers' just give up and become as bureaucratic as their elitist bosses.

Schools of Fish: Managing Change

As stated above, technology and customer needs change quickly. A school of fish provides a good illustration of what businesses need to become. The school swims together in the same direction until it senses danger. Within seconds the entire school turns and speeds in the opposite direction. Businesses must be able to change and adapt, becoming as fast and flexible as the school of fish.

Tomorrow's winners will be organizations lead by those who can manage the innovative ideas, dreams, and the natural problem-solving ability of people. Innovative leaders must transform the authority structure so everyone can contribute, feel part of the organization, and be able to contribute to the process. This involves breaking apart the hierarchy and pushing down decision-making responsibility to the lowest possible level. It involves aligning the entire organization on a definite course. It means focusing on the needs of customers or leading them toward a new direction or new way.

Motorcycle Management: Harley-Davidson

As a management consultant I am always on the lookout for exciting stories, particularly if these stories are about companies successfully making dramatic turnarounds. Fortunately, I have found one of those stories, a story about motorcycles.

Who could imagine an American motorcycle company providing an example of productivity, worker participation, quality, and pride of workmanship. To appreciate this dramatic transformation, you must appreciate where they came from.

In the 1980s, Harley-Davidson was a company in serious trouble. Everything that possibly could go wrong with a company went wrong. Like the red tide, competitive imports invaded American shores, swallowing a big share of the American market. During the 1980s, Japanese motorcycles cost less and were of higher quality.

This invasion had a devastating impact. The company was forced to lay off 40 percent of its workforce. Harley's financial lenders considered pulling the plug, dropping all financial support for the company. Harley was losing money for the first time in 50 years. The company had its back up against the wall, and the ship was sinking fast.

If the picture wasn't bleak enough, the company faced many other problems. Unlike today, the image of motorcycle riders, in the eyes of Americans, was a negative one. To complicate matters, the Harley-Davidson motorcycle suffered from severe mechanical problems. Harley owners had to place newspapers under the bike to contain all the oil leaks. The entire manufacturing process was full of problems, poorly organized, and outdated. For each bike manufactured, the result was thousands of dollars lost to rework, waste, and frustration. The revered Harley was spending more time in the shop than on the road. Like Humpty-Dumpty, the company had fallen off the wall and laid shattered on the ground.

The company was desperate—conventional management wisdom had failed. That is when they turned to their own workers for help. Front-line workers provided the ideas and energy putting Humpty-Dumpty back together again, staging one of the biggest corporate turnarounds in recent history.

From the manufacturing process to the marketing concepts, both workers and loyal owners helped to develop a brand new manufacturing process. Workers now controlled the assembly process, and management allowed workers to make decisions. Blue-collar workers formed teams and looked at innovative solutions, breathing life back into the manufacturing process. In one 30-day period, workers came up with $3 million worth of new innovative ideas for either reducing costs or improving performance. Furthermore, reducing inventory and going to a just-in-time assembly system resulted in even greater improvements.

The ending of this story resulted in a lot more than chrome and black leather. After several difficult and challenging years, Harley-Davidson increased profit by $59 million. They have captured 65 percent of the U.S. cycle market and presently can't keep up with demand. Today, quality is at an all time high, and Harley customer loyalty makes TV evangelists jealous. The image of the Harley rider has changed, too. The motorcycle, affectionately called a "Hog," now attracts people from all walks of society, spanning the globe, from CEO's and bank presidents to longhairs, crew cuts and everything in between.

Harley-Davidson learned a valuable lesson. Richard Teerlink, CEO of Harley- Davidson, gives full credit to his workers. He said,

> *Without the dedication of all its employees, no company can have long-term success. Top management must recognize that it has the responsibility and obligation to provide an environment in which an employee feels free to challenge the system to achieve success. Once the employee is committed, the techniques become easy.*

The final moral of this story should be clear to all of us. By capturing the ideas and natural problem-solving ability of the front-line worker, success is a lot easier. All the Kings horses and all the Kings men did put Harley-Davidson back together again.

Innovative Customer Service—City Government

Many state and local governments suffer from many of the same afflictions private corporations face today. Some of those afflictions include lack of space, mistrust, traditional leadership, rude and indifferent workers, bureaucratic rules and regulations, and the epidemic of shrinking budgets, to name a few. At the same time, citizens' expect more for less, and they want it yesterday!

Phoenix, Arizona, is the world's best managed city and a refreshing change from the above problems. Phoenix shows what a well-managed, well-led city government can do for its citizens and employees. Phoenix tied first place, winning the prestigious Bertelsmann Award for the best-managed city in the world. After a personal visit, I can see why they were selected.

Hanging on office walls all across the city is their vision statement and a set of "values" guiding the relationship between the city and the citizen.

VISION STATEMENT

Provide Excellent Customer Service and Consistent Policy Advice That Guides the Physical, Economic and Social Growth of Phoenix to Achieve a Better Quality of Life.

VALUES

- We believe that all groups should have equal access to the planning process to be able to influence decision makers on planning issues.

- We believe that citizens of the community must ultimately determine its vision and that the planners' role is to help them define it and work toward achieving it. The community's vision should be expressed in the general plan.

- We believe that planning should focus on actions that improve the quality of life for all in the community.

- We believe that planners must identify both the short-term and long-range impacts of planning decisions.

- We believe that we have a responsibility to provide excellent customer service.

- We believe in continual self-development to improve our skills and effectiveness.

Nowhere have I seen so many city employees so proud of what they do. These city employees view the citizens as their customers— amazing! This city has not fallen victim to short-sighted planning so many governments are guilty of. They created a dynamic environment that includes the latest in electronic information management services: city-owned television channels, smart cards, electronic cashiering, and numerous computer bulletin boards all with the goal of improving communication and access to the city government. Even their fire trucks are dispatched by satellite.

One of the most admirable accomplishments is their emphasis on building trust, trust between city government and citizen, and trust between city government and city government employee. Employees are given credit cards to reduce delays and bureaucratic request forms. So now, workers can go directly to any department store to buy nails, tools, and spare parts, thus speeding up projects. The result—citizens are happier, and the city reduces costs, inventory, and paper.

Here are a few of the other innovative practices and programs that pervade the best-managed city in the world.

→ **Bike on Bus Program.** All city buses have bike racks. One thousand commuters a day transport their bikes across the city.

→ **Library Computer Access.** All citizens with a home or office computer can access a computerized library catalog.

→ **City Hall Services.** Citizens no longer have to travel downtown to pay water bills, voter registration, make complaints, etc. Now the city provides these services in shopping malls and in some schools.

→ **Neighborhood News.** The city publishes a quarterly newsletter promoting healthy neighborhoods. Tips, facts, and other tidbits of community interest are printed in an upscale publishing format.

→ **Graffiti Busters**. A city sponsored group provides a 24-hour hotline and a team of people who can instruct and help remove graffiti off public property. Many businesses sponsored this program.

→ **City Volunteer Program**. The city organized an aggressive program using volunteers in the divisions of Parks and Recreation, libraries, police and fire departments, human services, etc. They even have volunteers collect, recycle, and distribute old bicycles.

→ **Electronic Access to the Phoenix City Council**. The city sponsors an electronic bulletin board listing all agenda items discussed by the council.

→ **Fire Services**. Fire trucks are dispatched by satellite. The city can monitor exact location of each fire truck and accurately dispatch the right type of equipment to each emergency location.

→ **Pre-Supervisory Development Program**. A series of courses are provided to city workers preparing for supervisory positions. Courses include basic principles of leadership, motivation, interviewing skills, delegation, and other management topics.

→ **Job Sharing**. City offers the ability to change full-time jobs into job sharing jobs. Employees can be reinstated back into full time status.

→ **Sick Child Care Program**. The City of Phoenix offers its employees in-home sick child care as part of their comprehensive child care program.

Who says government doesn't change with the times? The City of Phoenix gives new meaning to our Founding Fathers' original intent—"A government by the people, for the people."

Innovative Customer Service—Small Business

Though price makes an important difference between businesses today, it may not be the most important difference. Businesses can no longer compete strictly by having the fanciest advertising or by the price of goods and services alone. People are less willing to drive halfway across town to save $1.00. Today, the vast majority of urban dwellers would rather shop at a store, a bank, or any place that goes out of its way to serve them.

The recipe for exceptional customer service boils down to a few basic ingredients: flexibility, friendliness, speed, and exceeding customer needs and expectations—lots of little things making tremendous differences. If you are going to survive as a customer business, you need to provide unequaled customer service, no exceptions. The result will be greater satisfaction for both workers and customers, plus an exceptional bottom line.

Still Lake Nursery

Still Lake Nursery is a growing business. But much more is growing than plants. This is a family-owned business beginning with a few plants on a back porch—an American dream come true. This enterprise is managed by Garry and Gloria Still from Lawrenceville, Georgia. They successfully compete with the likes of Wal-Mart and the Pike's people. In fact, Still Lake is the largest retail grower in Gwinnett County, just outside Atlanta. You may recall that Gwinnett County was one of the fastest growing counties in the United States a few years ago.

Still Lake is a home-grown business. It began on the back porch of Garry and Gloria's home over 20 years ago. The first plants ended up at their small grocery store. People bought the plants and wanted more. The next year they built the first greenhouse, and the rest is history. Still Lake expanded from 4,000 to over 30,000 square feet. Today, many greenhouses cover the landscape, which includes a florist and a custom design shop.

On the human side of the business, Still Lake is filled with caring people who go out of their way to make a visit to Still Lake a memorable experience. Still Lake's success is built around the groundwork of treating customers right. Customer loyalty is as pervasive as the plants they grow. During the past 20 years this business blossomed strictly on word-of-mouth advertising—no advertising campaigns and silk glossies in the Sunday newspaper, no "digging in the dirt" radio commercials.

Garry and Gloria don't worry about competitors. Year after year, season after season, customers make their sojourn back to Still Lake for flower arrangements, poinsettias, hostas, and expert advice during weddings and compassionate care during funerals. They brag that one out of 10 customers for 20 years running still shops with them.

A successful business like this doesn't occur by accident. My time with Garry and Gloria helped me outline the following specific rules for growing a business:

→ **Provide high quality material.** There are no substitutes for quality. Reputation is critically important for growing a business. You want to be known for providing the best.

→ **Apply the 80/20 principle.** This old gem is still true today. Twenty percent of your customers generate 80 percent of your money. Focusing on this select group will generate a long-lasting and loyal clientele. I asked Garry what was the best thing he ever heard from one of his customers. He said not just one, but many of his customers say, "I'll see you in two weeks."

→ **Provide lots of information.** In the greenhouse business the customer wants to know as much as possible about the product. The information you provide is most often the major discriminator making or breaking the sale. To improve sales, forget selling things or a product. Instead, imagine you are selling information, and there just happens to be a plant or a product that goes along with it. People are willing to pay higher prices for extra service.

→ **Have access to lots of money.** Garry says it would be difficult to do what he did today. Don't start a business unless you can either borrow or have access to more money than you think you need. Believe me, you will probably need more than you think.

→ **Make it easy for customers to pay you.** Customers like to walk around and shop. But once they decide what they want, they are ready to go now. Have the cash registers and employees available to take their money and help them to the car—don't slow them down.

→ **Dare to be different.** You can't be all things to all people. Identify your "competitive advantage." What do you do best? Discover where do you stand out. Is it personalized service or do you provide a unique product or service? Are you available 24 hours a day? Whatever it is, your customers must identify you with that unique advantage.

→ **Go over and beyond.** Gloria manages the florist. Repeatedly, Gloria responds to customers' urgent needs for flower arrangements, particularly for the loss of a loved one. Tragedy never happens during normal business hours. On Friday nights and Sunday mornings, phone calls come in both at the florist shop and at their home. She even has worked on arrangements on Christmas day. It is sometimes inconvenient, but her customers know she can be counted on.

→ **Work Hard and Get Dirty.** High profits come from hard work. The majority of the people in this nation do not get rich quick—even in the Lotto. Successful businesses take years of hard work. Hours are long— 6 and 1/2 days a week, 12 hours a day for Garry and Gloria, especially during the spring.

CHAPTER 3

STANDING AT THE DOORSTEP OF OPPORTUNITY

CRISIS: A word originating from the Chinese, meaning, "Opportunity riding on a dangerous wind."

During a blistering summer evening in 1937, Fred Jones sat in his car near a lake in Minnesota. The heat was unbearable. He rolled down a window for a breath of fresh air. When he rolled the window down, his car filled with mosquitoes. Up the window went to keep mosquitoes out. Down the window went for some air. This cycle of opening and closing the window continued until he reached a point of total frustration. "Why doesn't somebody make a gadget to air-condition a car, like they do in theaters?" he said.

It Can't Be Done!

Fred Jones, an African-American, was forced to quit school when he was in the sixth grade to support his widowed mother. He was quite a handyman. His interests ranged from repairing automobiles and building race cars to constructing sound production equipment. His first involvement with air-conditioning began when he was employed at the Thermo-King Company.

Shortly after the mosquito episode, he drove to a library and studied everything available on air-conditioning and refrigeration. In those days air-conditioning for trucks and cars was deemed "impossible." Critics said, "It couldn't be done." Block ice was the only way to keep perishables from spoiling. This made long-term storage and transportation of food items extremely difficult and short-lived. Once his research was completed, he took out paper and drew the plan for the first mobile air-conditioning unit.

The next day didn't come quickly enough. He presented the plan to his boss. Joseph A. Numero was not interested—it was too radical an idea. Numero said, "It is too heavy ... too expensive, and I don't think anyone would buy it. Besides we're in the sound equipment business, so let's forget it."

The idea was shelved until a year later. Numero was playing golf with two other friends when one complained that one of his truck shipments of chickens had spoiled during a recent trip out of town. The entire shipment had to be thrown out and destroyed. On the golf course, the three men dared each other to invent a mobile air conditioner for trucks.

Numero remembered Jones' idea, but did not act on it. It wasn't until one of the golf partners called back to check on his progress that Numero called Jones in. Jones' idea sprung back to life, and his creative powers were released. In short order, Fred Jones, a man with only a sixth-grade education, finished his design for the first truck air conditioner. He used parts from a local junkyard.

This air conditioner quickly became a multimillion-dollar industry for the Thermo-King Corporation. Jones' innovative mind helped to create jobs for thousands of people, and the ripple effect had tremendous impact. His invention and spin-off products have kept food products fresh and available to people around the world.

Besides revolutionizing the food business with the mobile air conditioner, he continued to invent many items. Those driving cars today can credit Fred Jones for the air conditioner. He obtained somewhere between 35 to 50 patents for other inventions. The fruits his inventive mind included bicycles, hay loaders, broadcasting transmitters, and portable x-ray machines. He also invented the vending device that ejects movie theater tickets and change.

Years later he refined the truck air-conditioning system and created a refrigerator for storing blood products. He developed an air-conditioning unit for use in surgical hospitals during WW II. The same gasoline-powered air conditioner is still used today by the military to cool field hospitals. It also was used to calm honey bees during travel and to cool monkeys that flew in America's first space launches.

When Fred Jones retired, he had risen to Chief Engineer and Vice President of the Thermo-King Corporation. There are many people in this world who are born gifted, but few have risen to the heights of innovative success of Frederick M. Jones. A man from humble beginnings with only six years of education revolutionized the world we know today. His life was a testimony of how the power of ideas is strong enough to blur the lines of race, gender, and education, to overcome any disadvantage.

A World in Transition: Locomotive of Change

Not far from the county courthouse in Conyers, Georgia, stands the steam locomotive called "Dinky." It sits quietly, unmoved for the past several decades. The steam that once powered this engine is gone for good. Now, diesel locomotives speed past it on tracks heading in and out of Atlanta.

Alvin and Heidi Toffler provide some interesting thoughts about the changes we are experiencing in the world today. They see America changing from a "second wave," industrial economy to a "third wave," knowledge economy. America's "first wave" was the farming or agrarian economy that ended in approximately 1750. The second wave concluded around 1956. During this period, white-collar workers for the first time outnumbered blue-collared workers.

Like Dinky, the steam locomotive heralded the change in American society from the agrarian economy to the industrial economy. The microprocessor heralded the knowledge economy or what is commonly known as the information age. Now we see the initial stages of a new age I call "the techtronic age." Electronic tools have become as important as the information they are designed to manage.

Global Villages

The locomotive of change never seems to slow down; it only seems to get faster and faster. Issues we face in today's society are more complex, require greater flexibility, and demand quicker course corrections. Like the winds of a rushing hurricane, these changes impact our future, regardless of our position in society. It seems impossible to keep up with change, but the real issue is—are we even getting close? Are we as individuals and the businesses we work in going to be relevant and vital in the global village of the future? How are these changes going to affect our jobs, our families, and our standard of living? During this techtronic age, I see many trends developing.

Managing at the Speed of Light

Information technology has revolutionized how we work and live in the world today. As a child I remember watching the TV show, "Mayberry RFD," when Sheriff Andy had to ring Sarah, the telephone operator, to call Aunt Bee. Those days are long gone, and the television re-runs are fading fast in the archives of history. Every day a new, innovative product appears on the shelf, improving, processing, computerizing, and digitizing information faster than ever before. This poses great opportunities and also great challenges for both leaders and businesses.

Imagine, if you will, having breakfast at home in the morning. You switch on the PCTV (the heart of a computer and the screen of a television) and get a personalized electronic newspaper. The newspaper only includes the types of news you preselected—say, your updated stock portfolio, video highlights of your favorite sports teams, economic trends for the month to come, and what's new in Europe.

Sitting on the train to work, you check your Personal Digital Assistant (PDA) to get your e-mail. You send a fax to Bernie in Zurich and call your secretary to change an appointment. At your mobile office, you participate in a video-teleconference that spans the globe. Later you call Hilda, who customizes a software package for your client's meeting next week. You zap an entire slide presentation to send to Bernie in Zurich electronically. Back home, you unwind from your day's work. You decide to dial up "Gone With the Wind" from the pay-per-view movie library of 5000 films, only you change the ending and faces of the characters.

This little scenario is a present day reality. No longer is the world of computers the domain of computer "techies" or "wire heads." Managing in the information age becomes an environment where you are a part of a global community, where you manage your team members long distance, send electronic mail around the world, learn how to play cricket, get advice on starting a home-based business, read *Fortune* magazine, book a flight, and check out the weather in Sydney, Australia.

Information Revolution

Just consider how far we've advanced since 1912 when the Titanic struck an iceberg in the North Atlantic. The unsinkable ship sank in less than four hours, taking with it 1500 people to the bottom of the ocean. It was five days before New York City knew the exact details of this monstrous tragedy. Today, at CNN in Atlanta, it takes 30 seconds to air a major news story. Consider another story of how the Ventura County newspapers innovatively reported the news about the Los Angeles earthquake in 1994.

4:31 A.M.   A 6.6 Richter earthquake struck on January 17.

6:00 A.M.   Amid the confusion of the earthquake, Ventura County newspaper employees head to the office. Working with no power and only one phone line, managers decide to publish a special edition on the earthquake.

7:00 A.M.   Newsroom starts taking calls from reporters from their car phones. Newsroom lighted with a kerosine lantern, candles, and flashlights.

7:30 A.M.   The injured start arriving at local hospitals.

11:00 A.M.   Photos of the earthquake arrive 134 miles away at San Luis Obispo where the printing process begins. Cellular phones beam words and graphics to complete the special edition.

3:00 P.M.   Electricity is restored.

5:45 P.M.   A small plane delivers 20,000 copies of the special edition with some of the first photos of the devastation.

6:00 P.M.   Few, if any television stations and only a few radio stations are operating.

6:15 P.M.   Last issues of the newspaper delivered to local newsstands.

Survival of the Fit and the Fast

The survival of the fittest once depended on the biggest muscles and the strongest backs. The advantage may now go to the person who has the fastest computer, a modem, and who can master the latest version of Microsoft Windows. The information superhighway provides many people new opportunities.

Even Chinese restaurants are entering the information superhighway. In an advertisement in the Chinese Monthly, restaurant owners can customize their food menu and place it onto a floppy disk. Chinese restaurants can now hand their customers a computerized menu instead of a paper one. The menu is saved on a floppy disk. The disk is loaded onto the office computer revealing an interactive screen with all relevant information including how to contact the restaurant.

On the Internet, I discovered the home page for the first funeral industry on the information superhighway. Included in their home page is a photo of a $4,100 Montrachet solid mahogany casket.

This is what Carlos A. Howard Funeral Homes has to say about their funeral services:

> *Welcome to our on-line shop. We are pleased to be your full service Funeral Home on the Internet. We'll be providing Cyberspace travelers additional tips, hints, and suggestions for all their funeral arrangements.*

A group project by federal agencies now provides a one-stop link to government for business. President Clinton realized it is difficult for people to do business with the federal government. So now with a computer and access to the World Wide Web, you can get answers to questions, provide best practices, file documents with agencies, and solicit comments on regulations. Over 60 different federal agencies are available to provide help and assistance. The location of this site is: http://www.business.gov. You can also direct issues and concerns to the White House. Vice President Gore is even known to conduct on-line discussions on CompuServe.

Key Trends and Findings

Technology is one key opening the doors of future employment success. Fred Hofstetter in his book, *Multimedia Literacy*, says, "... multimedia is fast emerging as a basic skill that will be as important to life in the 21st century as reading is now...it is the use of a computer to present and combine text, graphics, audio and video with links and tools that let the user navigate, interact, create and communicate." The good news is that children can be effectively taught like never before. The bad news is most schools and classrooms still teach using the nineteenth century model of learning.

Disney World has dipped into the growing trend of learning vacations. Adults are no longer content just sitting around at the beach. In addition, growing numbers of senior adults are becoming more active than their predecessors. Adventure tours, continuing education, and working vacations are increasing in popularity.

The newly launched Disney Institute, "a $35 million center for learning vacations," will provide over 80 different programs lasting three or more days. These classes, mainly for adults, include everything from animation classes to gourmet cooking. Guest lecturers and instructors including resident artists and famous personalities will be on the agenda.

Cities like Atlanta and Phoenix have created "Electronic Neighborhoods" linking thousands of people electronically through an electronic architecture. Access Atlanta is a fee-for-service system designed to reach a new generation of people who have home computers. This service is a joint venture with the *Atlanta Journal-Constitution*, and Prodigy, an on-line service provider. Access Atlanta provides articles, information, current events, rapid transit maps and other information not available in the *Atlanta Journal-Constitution*.

The Phoenix developed the PhoenixNet concept connecting City Hall with the entire community. The infrastructure includes an e-mail system, smart cards, a central cashiering system, and electronic gateways to various entities. Instead of driving downtown to City Hall, citizens can now access the same services from their home computers.

High-Tech Military

The U.S. military is one of the most adaptable and innovative organizations in the world. The fall of the Berlin Wall and the evaporation of the Cold War has challenged military thinkers to figure out who, what, or where is the enemy? The Persian Gulf War highlighted the dedication of its service members and also its military superiority. On another front, service members are now spread throughout the country and abroad fighting a new type of battle. The battle is not with an enemy nation, but is called "Military Operations Other than War." These new operations include fighting forest fires, handling riots on the West Coast, providing aid and comfort to hurricane victims, and restoring order to Caribbean nations.

Boldly going where others have never gone before, the military is leading the way toward the twenty-first century with some of the most advanced technology available. Army leaders know that in the future, information will be as important as ammunition. The skills needed in battle are being sharpened not only at military training bases, but also in Silicon Valley and San Jose. Computers and advanced electronic equipment will allow soldiers to plan for and instantly see what is happening on future battlefields.

The Advanced Warfighting Experiment was field tested at Fort Irwin, California, the Army's high-tech training grounds. During this experiment, some warfighters were equipped with minicams mounted to their helmets. These minicams send real-time battle coverage back to military leaders. With real-time information, leaders can bring decisive fire power to bear on a scenerio, saving friendly lives and ending battles sooner.

A recent experiment in Haiti showed Pentagon officials how close they can actually get. A soldier in Haiti had a pen camera placed on his weapon. A satellite relayed live footage back to people in the Pentagon, who were able to watch every detail of the soldier's actions.

Medicine and Healthcare

The motto of the Army Medical Department is "Preserve the Fighting Strength." The Army Medical Department is heavily involved in new innovative ways to provide medical care. Army Surgeon General Alcide LaNoue has been one of the most innovative and visionary medical leaders in recent history.

In remote locations around the world, the availability of emergency medical treatment has always been limited. The medical department's focus has been to save the lives of as many soldiers as possible as soon after their injury as possible. Statistics show the first few minutes after injuries are the most critical. These critical moments mean life or death. To shorten this critical time period, the Army Medical Department has developed a worldwide network that can instantly send medical data and visual information around the world. This is done in many ways.

Telemonitoring. Soon standard issue for some soldiers will include several pieces of high-technology equipment. Some of these items include laptop computers, "Dick Tracy" type wristwatches, and special vests that monitor vitals signs such as blood loss, respiration, blood pressure, and body temperature. The special watch contains a Global Positioning Satellite (GPS) receiver that allows instant pinpointing of a location. Soldiers can no longer get lost in a firefight or on a night patrol. Additionally, soldiers who become separated from their unit or injured can manually activate the electronic signal. Airforce Captain Scott O'Grady used similar equipment to alert friendly forces after he was shot down over Bosnia. Soldiers will also receive smart identification tags that will replace the revered "dog tag." The smart tags will contain a microprocessor containing complete medical and dental records, personal information, and anything else that can be stored. When the tag is scanned into a computer, all information will be available to view on the screen. Thus, no more paper and lost records.

Teleconsultation. Miniature cameras and electronic transmitters are presently being used to transmit images and vital signs to medical base stations. The data and information is beamed across high-frequency radios back to physicians for instant triage, assessment, diagnosis, and advice on treatment. Physicians on the front line can be teleremoted to a major medical facility back in the United States. Now soldiers and civilians can receive the same high level of care in remote locations as they do back in the United States. This equipment has been successfully used on the border between Macedonia and Croatia. In another case, an orthopedist at Honolulu's Tripler Army Medical Center treated a foot for a patient located on the Kwajalein Atoll in the South Pacific. His treatment plan from 2,200 miles away avoided the amputation of his foot.

Telepresence Surgery. By combining virtual reality and robotics, surgeons can help perform operations hundreds of miles or even a continent away. In Canada, surgeons successfully performed gall bladder surgery on three patients. The surgeons performed the operation by manipulating a robotic arm in a remote location using a "Nintendo-style joystick." A robotic arm conducted the surgery while surgeons viewed the entire procedure through a video camera. No one assisted with the surgery. The three patients suffered "negligible" blood loss, and all three patients went home in less than 48 hours. Doctors said none of the patients experienced difficulty or anything more than "negligible" pain during the process. Researchers are now improving the robotic surgery by eliminating the need for a joystick and by using voice commands. The surgeon will regain the use of both hands and also gain more precise movements.

Virtual Reality. Military research and development personnel have created a virtual reality patient. Surgeons perform procedures on this "patient." Just like an actual patient, it bleeds, and tissues retract when an incision is made with the scalpel. It has the potential of reducing years off the time it takes to train surgical residents.

Telemedicine. Telemedicine is saving lives, providing improved medical access and saving money for both military and civilian patients around the country. The Medical College of Georgia has linked 25 houses where patients are monitored without leaving home. Savings are expected upwards from $15,000 to $20,000 for each avoided hospital stay. Telemedicine also provides an advantage by connecting larger hospitals with smaller, rural hospitals. Smaller, rural hospitals can now keep and care for an additional 50 to 80 percent of their patients. They no longer have to send them to larger, out of town hospitals for treatment. Telemedicine also provides doctors with a source of continuing education. Some specialists predict telemedicine will reduce health-delivery costs by 20 percent.

The Harvard Community Health Plan, an HMO, is allowing their customers who have their own modems and computers a special service.

Instead of spending the time driving in for treatment, they can communicate with the HMO over the computer any time during the day. For a minor problem, a simple treatment plan is sent to them via the modem. For more serious maladies, the HMO calls to set up an appointment.

Even though we are advancing technologically, we appear to lag behind in other important areas. This may be part of the transition process, the transition from the past to the future.

Present Day Realities

Along with the technological advances, there are some painful present day realities. As the following issues illustrate, we still are in a period of transition. By understanding the issues, we can better prepare ourselves for the future.

Workforce Diversity. Companies currently have workforces consisting of 20 percent minorities. Despite the growing numbers of females and minorities in the workplace, only 25 percent of these organizations are taking steps to train managers on how to manage diversity.

Gender Issues. Many businesses are concerned about the issues of female employees, but only a small percentage have done anything more than establishing a formal harassment policy, initiating supervisory training, and starting specific hiring programs. Meanwhile, a small but growing number of businesses are considering and starting to provide flexible benefits, including establishing on-site day care and sick and emergency child care services, mentoring, job sharing, and establishing women's support groups.

Aging Workforce. The workforce is getting older. At present, 35 percent of the workforce is made up of people over age 40. Estimates show those over age 65 will grow from 31.2 million in 1990 to 52.1 million in 2020. At Bethlehem Steel, the age of the average employee is 46 years old. By the year 2000, Bethlehem Steel could possibly lose 50 percent of their workforce to retirement.

Skills Shortages. Sixty-five percent of surveyed companies worry about not being able to find qualified workers. The same survey shows 42 percent are concerned about the gap between the skills employees have versus those needed to accomplish the job. The most common reason candidates are rejected is because of writing and verbal skills. Close to 60 percent of the businesses rejected candidates "most often." Another 36 percent say applicants have trouble adapting to the "work environment," and 10 percent fail to pass medical or drug testing. Of these new hires, 28 percent have either quit or been fired at the end of the first year. Reasons include absenteeism and inability to adjust to the work environment.

Lack of Trust. An *Atlanta Journal-Constitution/Southern Life* poll asked the question, "How would you rate the job performance of the following parts of the government?" Of the respondents, 80 percent feel the federal government is only doing a "poor or a fair job" running the country. In the same survey, the armed services got the highest ratings.

Another survey done by the Harris Poll shows Americans trust small business owners more than they do members of Congress or lawyers. Small business owners received a 64 percent positive rating while members of Congress landed a 19 percent rating. Here is how they rated:

> Small Business Owner: 64%
>
> Journalist: 39%
>
> Business Executive: 31%
>
> Lawyers: 25%
>
> Member of Congress: 19%

School Systems. Schools are getting failing grades, particularly regarding student dropouts. Each year there are 600,000 dropouts from schools across America. One out of every four dropouts ends up in jail. America's kids spend 180 days a year in class compared to 240 days or more for kids in Europe and Japan. Another report calls this a myth, reporting that by age 24, 85 percent of Americans have completed high school.

Working Harder and Getting Less. As children we were told, "if we work hard, we will get ahead." The new economy means less money for many people. Although America's economy is improving, most Americans' income has not increased for the past twenty years. How disheartening to realize the harder you work seems only to put you further and further behind. Higher paying jobs are becoming more difficult to find.

Many young adults can't afford to live on their own and for the first time, are earning less than their parents. There are 15 percent fewer families headed by adults under the age of 30 now than twenty years ago. During the past twenty years, the annual income of the adult male between the ages of 25 and 34 dropped by $8,300. This may explain why more and more young adults are returning to live with their parents.

Between 1987 and 1992, after adjusting for inflation, the average income of the American family dropped by more than $1,000. Families that only had the husband as the sole income producer dropped by $2,575. The cause, according to the *Atlanta-Journal Constitution* surrounds the loss of jobs in the mining and manufacturing industries.

Between 1983 and 1993, the nation lost approximately a million jobs in those two industries. At the same time, the nation experienced a 50 percent job increase in fast-food jobs, and a 45 percent increase in cashier positions. Janitors increased by 24 percent, and truck drivers gained a 22 percent increase. A recent letter in an Ann Landers column summarizes the feelings of many people.

> **Dear Ann Landers:** *Twelve years ago, I graduated from a major New England university with a high average. I come from a hard-working, blue-collar family. All I ever wanted was a home of my own and maybe a car and enough money to support a family.*
>
> *I am a hard worker and fast learner. I have never had a problem getting along with my bosses or the people I worked with in the computer industry. In the past 12 years, I've been laid off four times. (They don't call them layoffs anymore, they say "restructuring of the workplace").*
>
> *I have three part-time jobs because the trend is to replace every worker with two part-time workers. That way, the corporation doesn't have to offer benefits. I now work 60 hours a week and still have no medical benefits.*
>
> *I am 34. All I own is my car and my clothes. When my parents were my age, they owned a home and had two cars and three children.*

I am rapidly becoming disenchanted with corporate America. And there are thousands more like me.—Discouraged in Mass.

Dear Discouraged: *I hear you loud and clear. I also heard from an unprecedented number of readers in their 20s, 30s and 40s who share your views.*

Earning Depends on Learning

How much you earn may depend on how much you learn. Though the highest paid people are still those with college degrees, be careful to note that this trend is changing. In the future your employer may tie compensation to what you know and what you learn. Learning and education must continue beyond the "diploma mentality." Diplomas are becoming irrelevant in the techtronic age. The types of skills, not the number of diplomas, are the determining factors in earning a higher salary.

The 30 million highest paid Americans, who did not have a traditional four-year degree, obtained additional education after high school. This additional education either came from military service, technical school, or on-the-job training.

Robert Reich, the U.S. Secretary of Labor, predicts a 37 percent increase in technical jobs between 1990 and 2005. It is interesting to note that the DeVRY Institute of Technology stands out as one of the leaders in the field of technology-based education. They evaluate their educational programs based on the employers' needs, and they can graduate students with a bachelor's degree in only three years. Over the past ten years an impressive 90 percent of DeVRY's graduates were employed in their field within six months of graduation.

Crisis or Opportunity?

There are two ways to view these trends and information. You could view the negative information as a crisis. As a crisis, this brings both high amounts of frustration, fear, and possibly even anger. Or you can a more positive view—to see us as a nation in transition entering the doorstep of new opportunities. This positive view comes with the ability to see the opportunities within the crisis.

America is full of innovative people who can make the best out of a bad situation. I always remember the story about the Chinese merchant facing a crisis in Los Angeles. The merchant had established his business in Chinatown over twenty years ago when he faced the challenge of a lifetime.

For decades Won Chu faithfully served his community, providing an honest living for his family and himself. Everyone in Chinatown knew Won Chu as a living example of trustworthiness and success. His small shop was open six days a week from early in the morning to late at night.

One day a crisis appeared on the horizon. Two huge department stores bought the property on both sides of the small store. What was he going to do? How could he compete with modern retailers?

As fate would have it, both stores had simultaneous opening days. Each department store hung large signs over their doors. On the left side of Won Chu, a neon sign announced, "GRAND OPENING." On Won Chu's right, the competitor's sign said, "QUALITY MERCHANDISE."

Through the haze of chaos the Chinese merchant saw his one remaining chance. He ran to the back of the store, taking out a long piece of butcher paper and carefully began writing his own sign. He finished the project and quickly placed it above his small doorway leading into his shop. His sign said: "ENTER HERE!"

Won Chu knew the true meaning of crisis. In fact, the word originated from the Chinese. The word means, "opportunity riding on a dangerous wind." Won Chu saw the opportunity in this crisis, and he took it one step further. He took advantage of it.

Such people are called innovators. Innovators can see the opportunity in every crisis. They take advantage of the situation, either heading through the crisis or going around it. They don't stand still. They look at the facts, and they see the possibilities. Joel Barker calls these people "paradigm pioneers." A pioneer is a person who is a risk-taker, who can adjust and move into a new territory or a new way of doing something.

Innovators are people who:

→ Seek out new ideas and ways of doing things.

→ See beyond the crisis and see the opportunities.

→ Find new applications for old ideas.

→ See the world not for what it is, but what it could be.

→ Continually look at the outside to see what can be captured.

→ Build on success.

→ Will proceed over, around or through obstacles.

The old steam locomotive has served its purpose. A new locomotive is coming down the tracks. We are a nation in transition entering the doorstep of an exciting world full of opportunities. The opportunities before us are varied and dynamic. They involve global expansion and open markets with the free world, reinvention, and transformation of businesses. Standing before us lies the expansion of information highways, virtual reality, and the never-ending, ever-increasing technological advancement of products and services. Capturing these opportunities demands new ways of doing things. Now more than ever we need innovative leaders, and people capable of meeting the challenge to lead us to new vistas of opportunity.

CHAPTER 4

Meeting Bureaucracy
The Good, the Bad, and the Indifferent

"I think we have more machinery of government than is necessary, too many parasites living on the labor of the industrious."
—Thomas Jefferson, 1824

"If we do not halt this steady process of building commissions and regulatory bodies and special legislation like huge inverted pyramids over every one of the simple constitutional provisions, we shall soon be spending many billions of dollars more."
—F.D. Roosevelt, 1930

"Bureaucracy is an unnatural act committed by non-consenting adults."
—Sol Levitan, 1992

Rosabeth Moss Kanter, the editor of *Harvard Business Review*, identified four qualities businesses need to strive for. She says those businesses who want to be competitive must be:

→ fast,

→ focused,

→ flexible, and

→ friendly.

A "fast" business is one that can quickly adapt to the changing business environment. A "focused" organization is one that understands and adjusts quickly to changing customer needs and demands. A "flexible" organization is one not totally locked into a rigid, bureaucratic organizational structure. Its flexibility stems from an environment of teamwork and teams. It can build and disband teams as needed, capitalizing on the collective intelligence of the group. Finally, a "friendly" business is one that is cooperative and easy to work with. It is a place where workers want to come to work and where they can contribute to a mission. It is a place where customers and suppliers work side by side and have easy access to everyone within the organization.

Despite Mrs. Kanter's imperatives, there are far more organizations where the opposite holds true. There are more businesses where a traditional, "bureaucratic" attitude is the dominant management philosophy. Instead of being fast, focused, flexible, and friendly, they are slow, unfocused, inflexible, and unfriendly to work with and to work for.

The Art of Raising Hogs

The following letter describes the humorous side of a pathetic situation. Can a hog farmer make more money by not raising hogs? Some think there is a profitable case to be made, as evidenced by the following letter sent to the Secretary of the Department of Agriculture:

Dear Sir:

My friend, Ed Peterson, over at Wells, Iowa, received a check for $1,000 from the government for not raising hogs.

So I want to go into the "not-raising-hogs business" next year.

As I see it, the hardest part of this program will be in keeping an accurate inventory of how many hogs I haven't raised.

My friend Peterson is very joyful about the future of the business. He has been raising hogs for 20 years or so, and the *best he ever made on them was $420 in 1968, until this year, when he got your check for $1,000 for not raising hogs.*

If I get $1,000 for not raising 50 hogs, will I get $2,000 for not raising 100 hogs? I plan to operate on a small scale at first, holding myself down to about 4,000 hogs not raised, which will mean about $80,000 the first year.

Now another thing, these hogs I will not raise will not eat 100,000 bushels of corn. I understand that you also pay farmers for not raising corn or wheat. Will I qualify for payments for not raising wheat and corn not to feed the 4,000 hogs I am not going to raise?

Also, I am considering the "not-milking-cows business," so please send me any information on that, too.

In view of these circumstances, you understand that I will be totally unemployed and therefore plan to file for unemployment and food stamps.

Patriotically yours,

John C. Cramer

This letter illustrates exactly what we don't want in our business systems. This is not a slam on farmers or food subsidies, but it is an example of an out of control "bureaucratic mindset." We don't want a system that rewards people for doing the wrong things.

Bureaucracy: Myth and Reality

The word "bureaucracy" is an emotional word bringing forth both positive and negative feelings. Decades ago, to be called a "bureaucrat" was a positive comment. Today it has an entirely different connotation.

There are many myths and perceptions about bureaucracy. It is far more popular to condemn it without giving it fair scrutiny. It is easier to say it is inefficient and obsolete instead of looking at its virtues. I hope to level the playing field and objectively evaluate both the myths and reality surrounding bureaucracy and the bureaucratic organization.

MYTH 1:   BUREAUCRACIES ARE HEADED FOR EXTINCTION.

Many theorists think bureaucracies have served their purpose, and like the dinosaurs, will fade away. Not true. The truth is a bureaucracy is neither good nor bad; it is only a form of organizational structure. The word bureaucracy traditionally represents a type of hierarchical organizational structure. It is not suited for all types of organizations, but is best suited for large organizations that must control power and manage resources.

Bureaucracy exists in almost every organization, in various extremes, no matter the size of the organization. Bureaucracies existed from the ancient Roman Empire to the present day Catholic Church and will probably be around much longer. We make a mistake when we allow organizations to become overly "bureaucratic." Even bureaucracies can be come overly bureaucratic. This means too rigid, too inflexible, and too out of touch with both its employees and reality. This is bad. When the customer-oriented, information-based, profit-oriented business becomes bureaucratic, then extinction is inevitable. Extinction is inevitable from two sources:

→ **Competitors and**

→ **Tools of technology**

Competition is still the great equalizer. Competition means there are other businesses that can do things faster, better, and cheaper. Even the military has competition of sorts. From the military perspective, the "enemy" is out there that could be faster, better, and more lethal.

The other factor leading to extinction is the tools of technology. In the techtronic age, the advance of technology negates the need for overly bureaucratic organizational structure. In the past, we needed layers of managers to control information. Now computers and information systems minimize the need for all this structure.

MYTH 2:   A BUREAUCRACY NO LONGER SERVES A PURPOSE.

A bureaucracy is a unique type of organization serving a particular purpose and a particular function. Its specific purpose surrounds the command and control of people and the organization and distribution of resources. In fact, it is far superior in performing these special functions than any other organizational structure.

A bureaucracy is an organizational structure that controls and projects power. Control and power are established by a top-down management structure. I'm quick to emphasize that all organizations are not suited for the bureaucratic organizational structure. Businesses create problems by matching the wrong organizational structure with the wrong type of business.

Different types of businesses need different types of management structures. A team working on developing a software program does not need authority, and command and control to accomplish the task. A technology-based, team-oriented structure must be flatter and more self-directed. A less structured, more creative approach would be desired. The typical bureaucratic structure would severely limit and hinder performance in this type of industry.

However, the federal government, the military, or other large organizations' main purpose is to control power and organize resources. To use a bureaucracy to manage Microsoft would be totally inefficient. Within days they would be out of business. Using a Microsoft style of management to run the military would likewise be disastrous.

The effectiveness or ineffectiveness of the organizational structure is decided by its results. The results of the organization are determined if it can efficiently accomplish its goals and meet the needs of the customer in a timely manner.

In summary, a bureaucracy serves a specific purpose and is not the best structure for all organizations. It is not going away and is going to exist until we find a better way to manage large organizations.

MYTH 3:   A BUREAUCRACY IS UNPRODUCTIVE, WASTEFUL, AND INEFFICIENT.

As we said earlier, a bureaucratic organization is not the best suited organizational structure for all purposes. This is particularly true in an organization that must rapidly adapt to change and depends on the free flow of large quantities of information. If that is true, then a bureaucracy may not be the best choice. Contrary to popular opinion, bureaucracies can still be innovative and creative. Elliott Jaques, coauthor of the book, *Executive Leadership*, feels:

> *"that managerial hierarchy is the most efficient, the hardiest, and in fact the most natural structure ever devised for large organizations. Properly structured hierarchy can release energy and creativity, rationalize productivity, and actually improve morale."*

Jaques goes on to say that most hierarchies are not maximizing their potential. Dr. Edwards Deming would say we are not "optimizing the system." Instead of organizing around goals and the mission, bureaucracies are organized "to accommodate pay brackets and facilitate career development instead."

According to Jaques, to optimize the bureaucratic system, managers need clear goals. He outlines **three important roles of the manager:**

1. The first and most important role is that managers have to add value to work and be held accountable for their subordinate's work.

2. The second role is that managers must be held accountable to create a team environment for this work.

3. Finally, managers must be held accountable for setting directions and getting workers to follow enthusiastically.

MYTH 4: PEOPLE WITHIN A BUREAUCRACY ARE MINDLESS INCOMPETENTS.

The most dedicated people I have known worked within bureaucracies. My experience showed me there were more patriotic, loyal, and hard-working people attracted to the military and government service than anywhere else. These people I worked with enjoyed service—helping people. To label them anything less than professional would be unfair and inaccurate.

Unfortunately, good people get swallowed by a bad system. An overly bureaucratic organization takes on a life of its own. An overly restrictive, rank-oriented mentality harms individual initiative. It depersonalizes people. The result—excellent people become trapped in a bad system.

Duty, Honor and Country. Over the years I've held many leadership positions in the military. Over the course of those same years, I've worked with many outstanding and dedicated people in both the military and federal civil service. The memory of one person stands out clearly in my mind.

Gail was an administrative assistant who worked with me at Fort Benning, Georgia. She was one of the hardest working people I knew. She was always at the office early and would stay until she was no longer needed. She worked harder and longer than many soldiers assigned to our unit.

On occasion, we would talk about why we both decided to work for the federal government. She told me she joined the Civil Service because she wanted to serve the country, and this was the best way she knew how.

Months later my stepfather became ill, suddenly passing away. I was out of the office many miles away in a meeting. Gail took the call from my sister and drove her car across the military base and found me. Quietly entering the room, she touched my arm, telling me the bad news.

Gail had many options before her. Instead of driving across the base, she could have used a telephone and called me at the meeting. She could have sent a driver with a note, but she personally assumed the painful mission. The remainder of the day was blurry, but what she did for me that day will never be forgotten.

Gail typifies the type of person who works for the government. They joined to serve the country and to make a difference. I could fill the pages of this book with stories of dedication and patriotism. Many times the media is all too quick to create sensational headlines about those few who are either crooked or make mistakes. All the while, dedicated people work quietly and professionally behind the scenes doing what is right.

The Traditional Bureaucracy

Bureaucracy takes many forms—good, bad, and indifferent. We are all familiar with the traditional form of bureaucracy with its labyrinth of rules, regulations, hoops and hurdles, and restrictive command and control. This is what I call the traditional bureaucracy.

The traditional view of bureaucracy is a management system based on control and designed upon a hierarchical structure. In the broader sense, the traditional bureaucracy goes beyond just a hierarchical management structure. The negative aspects are far more serious than most people realize.

Bureaucracy affects peoples' thinking. It becomes a top-down mental attitude approach of doing business. This bureaucratic attitude is harmful, and it can become a debilitating disease. It limits peoples' ideas and innate potential. It can rob pride from people, treating workers as if they are incapable of thinking and unable to make decisions.

Often a traditional bureaucracy forces people into two distinct classes—those who think and those who don't. In more specific terms, those who are in charge, who have all the ideas, and enforce the rules, along with those who must follow the rules and carry out the ideas of those in charge. I think this is what the late Dr. Edwards Deming had in mind when he made the following comment: "We are all born with intrinsic motivation, self-esteem, dignity, an eagerness to learn. Our present system of management crushes that all out."

The philosopher, Max Weber, wanted to perfect the bureaucracy into a complete and comprehensive management system. In his early writings, he highlighted the "dehumanizing" characteristic of bureaucracy, saying, "the goal of any complex organization should be to minimize—indeed, eliminate—individual behavior that is contrary to the responses desired by the organization." It was his goal to design a system that minimizes human interaction. This mentality is still present today in many organizations across the world.

Bureaucracy: Symptoms of a Debilitating Disease

There are many reasons to be critical of the traditional bureaucracy. A traditional bureaucracy is not the best form to create an innovative environment. Typically, the traditional bureaucracy resists innovation.

How do you know if you work in an overly bureaucratic organization? A skilled business leader can diagnosis the symptoms and treat accordingly. Here are several symptoms.

1.   A REGULATORY-BASED CULTURE, NOT A PEOPLE-BASED CULTURE.

Vice President Gore said, "Sometimes it seems to me that the whole federal government is organized in the vain pursuit of preventing anyone from making a mistake." The traditional bureaucracy is structured around rules, regulations, and policies. We must be asking ourselves, "Do we need all these policies and procedures. Do we need to create a new rule every time something goes wrong?" An organization with no rules would be irresponsible. On the other hand, an over-regulated environment hurts initiative and individual creativity.

2.   CENTRALIZED DECISION MAKING.

The traditional bureaucracy has a top-down decision-making process. Ideas, projects, and decisions must be pushed up the chain

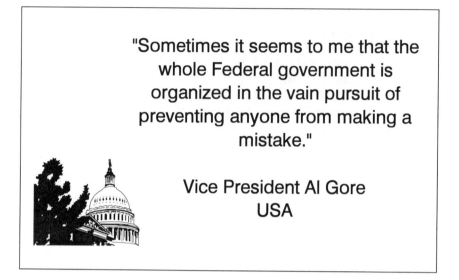

"Sometimes it seems to me that the whole Federal government is organized in the vain pursuit of preventing anyone from making a mistake."

Vice President Al Gore
USA

of command for approval. If approved, the decision finally cascades back down for action.

Bureaucracies often substitute a form of passive management for true empowered leadership. Passive management includes what is commonly know as "staff work." People who do staff work manufacture staffing papers, decision papers, and briefings, all unconsciously designed to inform and enable the centralized decision maker the ability to make centralized decisions. Decisions that should take minutes take weeks and months. In a fast-changing environment this spells disaster.

Many times this centralized decision-making process creates additional problems. When you have to climb a mountain for a decision, people decide it is easier to avoid the climb all together. People would rather ignore important issues than fight the system. The result is an organization paralyzed by its own ineffectiveness.

IBM has done many things well. However, much criticism has been leveled at IBM because of its bureaucratic decision-making process. In 1990, IBM had a chance to buy a portion of Borland International for $10 a share. Borland is a successful software design company. The IBM executive who was responsible for working the deal had to go through a detailed process to get permission to buy the stock. Weeks later, he finally got the go-ahead, but the stock had risen to $87 a share, losing several million dollars of profit potential. After that frustrating experience, the executive refused to go through the approval process again—so he dropped the whole idea. As one IBM business partner described, "trying to get action out of IBM...is like swimming through giant pools of peanut butter."

3.   DIFFICULTY IN FIXING MISTAKES.

One of the jobs I had in the Army was the Director of Innovation for the Army Medical Department. I was enthusiastic about my job and tried to help as many people as possible. One day I asked a surgeon the following question: "What have you done innovatively lately?" He frowned and said something I'll never forget: "Innovative! You know it is easier for me to take two x-rays of my patient than try to find the original!"

His answer still reverberates in my mind. His answer meant twice the cost, twice the number of trips to the hospital, two baby-sitters, twice the filing time for the x-ray department, and a patient exposed to twice the amount of radiation. How costly was this problem? It only represented the tip of a massive iceberg! Why was it easier to take a second x-ray than try to fix the problem?

In a bureaucratic organization, the people at the top of the organization have the responsibility for interpreting and approving any changes to regulations. This slows decision making because the responsibility and power to make decisions is taken away from those who need it the most. The ones who need it the most are usually the ones closest to the customers, closest to the action. This is why bureaucracies have difficulty fixing mistakes. The authority for exceptions and changes to the rules has been removed from those who need the power to improve the situation. The larger the organization, the longer it takes, "So...why try to fix the problem. They'll never understand the problem anyway. If you say something about it, they will put you in charge of the problem!" The bureaucratic system rewards people for not rocking the boat and maintaining status quo.

4.   RESISTS CHANGE.

Traditional bureaucracies resist change. Bureaucracies are compartmentalized, and functionally aligned, department by department. The people within the departments have specialized job descriptions focusing on narrow subject areas. Because of this specialization, change becomes difficult. It takes a crisis to make a significant change in a bureaucracy.

A crisis is a necessary evil in the bureaucratic change process. With the right leadership and the right crisis, a bureaucracy will achieve a high level of performance. Furthermore, the crisis must be of such significant proportions that there are no other alternatives. Otherwise, inertia remains a more powerful force.

When Saddam Hussein moved into Kuwait, it set off one of the largest military operations in history. Operation Desert Storm was a hallmark for the U.S. military. More soldiers, sailors, airmen, marines, federal workers, and contractors mobilized and moved out unlike any previous military operation. Around the clock, equipment was loaded on ships, and aircraft heading to the Middle East.

This crisis stimulated a high level of performance. What normally would have taken weeks and months through normal procurement and contracting processes took hours and days. The government changed and modified the rules and regulations to speed up the process. No time in history were there so many people and so much equipment moved across the world in such a short time. However, when victory was won and when everything and everyone moved back home, everything went back to normal. The same bureaucratic rules and procedures returned. Today, it takes months to order a training video because of the immense procurement process. The moral of the story is—to change a bureaucracy, the organization needs two elements: a crisis and the right kind of leadership.

A bureaucracy has its own self-protecting mechanism. The rule-based organization creates more rules and regulations to prevent change. Like a lizard that grows back its tail, once the crisis is over, everything goes back the way it was.

5.   DEFINED PECKING ORDERS.

Within the traditional bureaucracy, people assume certain characteristic behaviors. In its worse form, a bureaucracy almost becomes a caste system. Hierarchical layering dictates what roles to take, who to talk to, and who to associate with. These are unwritten rules, but nonetheless, are clearly defined to those who work within the organization. There are exceptions to the pecking orders, but they usually occur only briefly during special events, such as annual picnics and company events, and with certain people.

For an organization wanting innovation, this is a major impediment. In the innovative organization, people must feel they have equal access to all people, to all levels of the organization. The role of the leader is to break down the barriers and create this environment. In the traditional bureaucracy, one of the following organizational roles of behavior usually occurs:

→ **Ceremonialists**

→ **Activists**

→ **Escapists**

→ **Innovators**

→ **Technical Experts**

The *ceremonialist* is one of the roles of behavior within the traditional bureaucracy. A ceremonialist is a person who has made a lifelong commitment to the system. Safety and security are obtained by conformity to the traditions and customs of the organization. Ceremonialists have been assimilated by the system. Though frustrated at times, they may choose to support instead of trying to fight, change, or improve the system. This may be particularly true of those who have risen to a high level of authority and position.

The ceremonialist may even resent those who try to change the organization—the innovators. They spend a great deal of time trying to normalize the organization and those within it. Ceremonialists may protect the system by creating more rules and procedures to further insulate and protect their positions.

The *activists* are like worker bees in the hive. They are the ones who do the real work within the bureaucracy. Over the years they have become adept in working around the system. Going around the bureaucracy is a lot easier than trying to work within it. Ceremonialists think decisions are made in briefings and formal meetings. On the other hand, activists know who makes the decisions and how the decisions are made. Quietly and efficiently, they go about obtaining important decisions in hallways, restrooms, gyms, and other informal gatherings.

The *escapist* is another role of behavior. These people possess strong feelings about their work environment. They feel because the environment, with its impersonal and restrictive rules, is too difficult to make a difference, they don't try. When faced with no hope of change or no hope of reward or recognition, escape becomes the logical alternative. Why try to make a difference when no one seems to care? Escapists have their own unwritten rules that say,

→ Don't raise your hand.

→ Don't volunteer.

→ Don't take risks.

→ Wait to be told what to do.

→ Average performance is good enough.

People have a tremendous capacity for achievement. When people can't reach their potential on the job, they divert their energy and potential to other activities and relationships. Those people who aren't fulfilled at work devote time and energy to community affairs, theater, and other outside activities. They may use their job to write books, participate in "coffee-club" socials, and other forms of creative expression.

The key point to realize is that people want to contribute in a meaningful way. If they can't do on the job, they will go elsewhere. It is the leader's job to try to capture as much of their potential as possible. Not just for the benefit of the business, but for the benefit of the individual.

Today we need more innovators and people willing to take a "proceed until apprehended" attitude. By ignoring outdated, outmoded rules and regulations, we can turn back the stifling bureaucracy and do the right thing. These people form the creative energy and the changing force in the "new bureaucracy."

Another role is the *technical expert*. This person, by virtue of their technical expertise, manages to access and cross all levels of the strata. A technical expert appears in many shapes and sizes. Most commonly, they appear as computer technicians who repair computers and computer systems. Their unique authority stems from their technical expertise. Whether it is the office of the CEO or the Commanding General, this person can enter all doors. They don't threaten the authority of those in power. These people go about their business quietly maintaining the organizational structure.

The *innovator* is an interesting character. They are always in the minority, but fulfill an important role in the bureaucratic system. Innovators take personal pride in going around the system to accomplish their goals. I think innovators see themselves as Robin Hood, stealing from the rich to help the poor. The poor in this case are the lower-ranking people who work within the bureaucracy, stifled by the rules and regulations. Innovators have a "proceed until apprehended" attitude. Innovators discriminate between the dumb rules and those that are necessary.

The innovator is both admired and sometimes, held in contempt. This person's behavior is viewed as rebellious and threatening, particularly by the ceremonialists. Innovators see themselves serving as catalysts for positive change. They want to do the right thing. If we remember the wall of bureaucracy described in Chapter 1, the innovator is the one who helps create the cracks in the wall.

Gammon's Law—Theory of Bureaucratic Displacement

I first heard Dr. Max Gammon speak at a conference sponsored by the Army Medical Department several years ago. He is a physician living in London, England. His research and experience with socialized healthcare in Britain gives new insight about the effect of bureaucracy, not only in the healthcare field, but in business.

Prior to 1948, healthcare in Great Britain was managed by independent general hospitals, asylums, and teaching hospitals. Management practices at that time were informal and people oriented. These hospitals and clinics successfully managed themselves using leaner administrative staffs.

World War II showed the British government needed a more centralized control over hospitals and medical services. In 1948 Britain created the National Health Service (NHS). The NHS owned 544,000 hospital beds in 1948. In 1973 the number of hospital beds dropped down to 491,000. Between 1948 and 1990, the number of available hospital beds fell from 10 beds per thousand people to 5.6 beds per thousand. During that period, 450,000 additional employees were hired. The greatest increase of employees was in administrative staff, a whopping 75 percent increase. This increase represented people who had little or nothing to do with treatment and the care of patients. In fact, according to Dr. Gammon, these administrative jobs "displaced and obstructed" patient care.

So, what was the result? The system became overly bureaucratic. Waiting time increased, and access to the system became terribly difficult. Great Britain has one million people waiting up to two years for "non-urgent" procedures, including such procedures as hernia treatment, hip replacements, and prostatectomies. Waiting six months for a dental procedure is not uncommon.

Dr. Gammon's own patients have suffered due to the bureaucratic system in Britain. The shortage of hospital beds forced one of his patients, who was two weeks overdue with a complicated pregnancy, to have her baby in her bathroom. The baby died before she could get to the hospital. A 72-year-old man waited a year for surgery to correct his bladder obstruction. He went into complete urinary retention. Upon arrival at the hospital, he was

GAMMON'S LAW

The Theory of Bureaucratic Displacement:

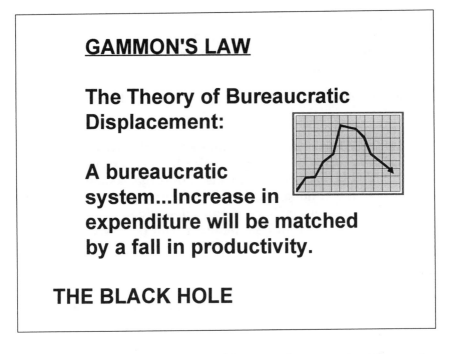

A bureaucratic system...Increase in expenditure will be matched by a fall in productivity.

THE BLACK HOLE

given a catheter and discharged the next day to wait at home for a hospital bed.

Hear That "Sucking Sound"

Dr. Gammon created the Theory of Bureaucratic Displacement or what is commonly known as "Gammon's Law." Part of the theory included a mathematical formula measuring the difference between healthcare input and output. For the input, he took the number of people employed by the NHS and used the number of hospital beds as the output. In corresponding fashion, the hospital beds decreased while the numbers of administrative staff, rules, regulations, and the system inflexibility increased.

Dr. Gammon has strong feelings about NHS and used medical terminology to describe the growth rate of administrative staff. He said it was like an "explosive enema." His view supports the feeling that the "business of bureaucrats is delaying the business of productive people."

There is a phenomenon that occurs with the bureaucratization of any system. It occurs in all organizations or any system, whether it is healthcare, public education, or government. There are two laws within the phenomenon, two distinct, inevitable reactions.

Law 1: **An increase in spending will be matched by a fall in productivity.**

Law 2: **When resources become limited, the bureaucratic portion of the organization begins to cannibalize the productive elements of the organization, (e.g., fewer hospitals, fewer healthcare providers, but greater numbers of non-value added administrative staff, offices, auditors, and paperwork).**

Economic Black Holes

This process creates what Gammon calls "economic black holes." In a bureaucratic system, "survival is not dependent on performance." When there is no competition, bureaucracy grows like cancer. No competition breeds inefficiency and waste. Because of inefficiency and waste, bureaucrats add more administrative staff to help stop the waste and inefficiency. Someone has to pay for all the administrative staff, so more and more money is sucked into the black hole. In return, for every dollar that goes in, there is a decrease in productivity. To feed all the bureaucratic elements, healthcare systems must raise prices. Higher prices result in more regulations, more control, and more supervision. Because healthcare costs more, the problem of increased costs is solved by cutting back staff. The staff that gets cut are usually people providing care to patients. Now, who is taking care of the patient? Patients get mad. Patients hire lawyers. Lawyers sue hospitals. More administrative staff is added, and on and on it goes—a vicious circle. The result is an organization that becomes more concerned about meeting requirements and rules than providing quality healthcare.

The New Bureaucracy

I am seeing more evidence of a new trend emerging from the ashes of the traditional bureaucracy. Throughout the world, we are seeing a new growth of dynamic leaders and innovators replacing the traditional "status quo" mindset. It is what I call the "new bureaucracy."

The new bureaucracy enters the twenty-first century with new creativity and a new, reformed style of leadership. A new bureaucracy is one that has an innovative orientation of adding value and serving its customers or citizens. *Innovation*, simply put, **is the ability to implement new ideas, services, products, and processes.** In other words, the ability to adapt to the changing environment.

Programs and philosophies such as Total Quality Management, teams, reengineering, and "Reinventing Government" efforts have helped transform the "old style" of management into a leaner, more effective form of management. Cities and governments, such as those in Phoenix, Atlanta, Charleston, and Hampton, Virginia, are leading the way. The innovative efforts of the military have put it on the forward edge of technology developments. Here are a few characteristics of the new bureaucracy.

MARCHING ORDERS FOR THE NEW BUREAUCRACY

→ Changes and adapts based on the organization mission.

→ Continuously improves all products and services.

→ Measures performance.

→ Establishes more leadership and less management.

→ Focuses on serving customers.

→ Creates offices and departments that add value.

→ Promotes people on performance, not just longevity.

→ Encourages doing things differently.

→ Minimizes negative influences of titles, rank, and rigid structure.

→ Gives people permission to stop doing dumb things.

CHAPTER 5

INNOVATIVE LEADERSHIP: STEERING THE SHIP

"Troops can't be managed into battle. They have to be led."

—Napoleon

The critical factor needed in all organizations today is leadership. Now, more than ever, we need passionate leaders, who, like ice breaker ships, can chop through bureaucratic icebergs, courageously charting a new course, not protecting the past. Such people are called innovative leaders.

As traditional walls crumble, the base of power changes. Where once leadership was a role based on position and status, we now see a whole new set of forces that comprise leadership. Leaders must regain those same pioneering characteristics and the fearless determination that made America the most powerful and most innovative country in the world. The true test of successful leadership is taking the right actions leading people to the right destination.

Once upon a time, leadership was a simple process. All that was needed was to not rock the boat, not make waves, and give a few orders, and everything would work out. Silently, and unintentionally, we've built bureaucracies that substituted leadership with a form of passive management, satisfied with maintaining the status quo, locked in inertia. We got comfortable with our old styles of management, forgetting the importance of searching out the ideas of people. Rigidity, structure, and position have replaced initiative to do what is right.

The business environment of the twenty-first century will not resemble anything we've seen. Rank, position, and one's place on the hierarchical pyramid is rapidly becoming less important. The bureaucratic organizational chart of the previous era is collapsing. Growing in its place is a more flexible organization that can expand and contract on demand. Replacing structure and control is a variety of self-directed work teams and a quiltwork of individuals telecommuting from all points of the compass.

The Lights Are On But Nobody's Home

The past decade has left an indelible mark on America's workforce. In the United States, 9 million people have lost jobs due to layoffs, restructurings, and business failures. Only half of the original 1980 *Fortune* 500 companies remained on the list in 1990. As a result, people lost their jobs because the companies they worked for failed to do their homework. That homework included responding to inside and outside pressures impacting on their industries.

Competitive pressures were coming from both inside and outside America. First, there were competitive forces from the outside. Products from other countries arrived on our shores which cost less and were of higher quality. It seemed like overnight, Americans were buying foreign-made cars, VCRs, computer chips, and other consumer items by the truckload. On "Main Street America," manufacturers stared at warehouses full of expensive and outmoded, American-made products.

Pressure from inside the country pulled us in another direction. Trends changed, our workforce became more demanding and more expensive. Wage hikes and greater benefits negotiated by

unions continued to spiral out of proportion. Increasing government and state rules and regulations placed tighter and tighter
restrictions on businesses. Profit margins narrowed, and American
businesses took their factories overseas in search of large workforces
who would work for low wages. America almost put itself out of
business. We've been our own greatest enemy.

More Leaders Needed

A *leader* is a **person who inspires people to take a journey to
a destination they wouldn't go to by themselves.** Today, more
than ever we need people who breathe new life into organizations
and take them places they wouldn't go to by themselves. To get an
organization to take a journey, to change from old ways to new
ones, requires a new style of leadership.

Rapid changes in technology, overseas competition, deregula-
tion, fragmentation of markets, and increasing diversity of the
workforce are all forcing companies to adapt quickly to new circumstances. Changes in the business environment were once or-
derly and incremental. They are indiscriminate and much more
dramatic now. Peter Drucker puts it bluntly by saying, "Every
organization has to prepare for the abandonment of everything it
does." This situation calls for more than managers—it requires
leaders. The two are by no means synonymous. The following table
shows the main differences between the functions of mangers and
leaders

MANAGER	LEADER
Carries out planning and budgeting	Charts a course providing direction
Oversees organizing and staffing	Provides guidance and counsel
Follows orders	Encourages people to follow their example
Controls and solves problems	Motivates and inspires
Maintains control and order	Creates an environment for change
Protects status quo	Builds relationships and trust
Writes memorandums	Trains and teaches
Follows rules and regulations	Questions rules and regulations

The Traits of an Innovative Leader

Leaders do not gain their positions merely through appointment, but through the free acceptance of their leadership by subordinates. Many people believe that managers can automatically become good leaders. Others believe that people are born natural leaders. These two statements can't be further from the truth. While the most influential leaders seem to have a charismatic talent, almost anyone can learn how to become a better leader. It takes a lot of work and commitment, but the results are extraordinary. There are nine traits leaders seem to share:

1. **They have a mission.** The greatest leaders have a defining mission in their life. This mission is called many things—a purpose, an obsession, or a calling. What it is called is unimportant. What is important is that this mission, above all other traits, separates managers from leaders. Leaders stand for something.

2. **They create a vision.** A clear picture of the future goal will help the achievement of it. Steve S. Chen left Cray Research because he had a vision of a super computer that Cray decided not to build. Chen's vision and conviction were so potent that forty co-workers left with him. He was able to sell his vision, which can be difficult.

3. **They trust their employees.** With the diminishing influence of the command-and-control structure, responsibility is pushed down through the ranks to rely on the ideas and energies of all workers. This delegation of authority requires that employees have a voice in the decision-making process, which takes away some of the manager's power and control.

4. **They keep their heads in a crisis.** Leaders take a position and defend it when things go awry. Being graceful under fire is the surest way to building credibility.

5. **They encourage risk taking.** If a company does not examine new ways of doing things, if it does not push its boundaries, if it never makes mistakes, it will not be competitive. Leaders resist the safe road and allow others to take chances. That does not imply indiscriminate experimentation.

6. **They are experts.** Good leaders are intimately familiar with their company's products and services. August Bush of Anheuser-Bush knows everything there is to know about making beer. Again, it is a question of establishing credibility. Employees know immediately when a superior is 'winging it,' and they stop listening.

7. **They know what is essential.** Leaders have a remarkable ability to zero in on what is important. They can simplify complex problems elegantly without taking the easy way out.

8. **They listen.** Ever wonder why we have two ears and only one mouth? The greatest leaders are those who truly listen. They listen to peoples' ideas, concerns, and problems. The leader's job is to listen to everyone and everything.

9. **They are teachers and mentors.** In our rapidly changing environment, organizations must create a learning environment. The senior people must be teaching and training junior people. We are not necessarily talking about formal classroom training. We need leaders talking to people in hallways, in the restaurants, everywhere. Everyone should be mentoring someone else.

Passionate Leadership

Innovative leaders span a narrow gap between two key areas: passion for action and passion for people. A bold orientation for action matched with compassion for people creates an emotional energy transforming bureaucracies into innovative and energetic enterprises. The past decade has damaged the motivation and morale of the workforce. Many businesses and organizations have a workforce that is skeptical and distrustful of the management structure. They feel cheated and betrayed. It will take compassionate leaders to heal the wounds caused by both the past actions of careless management and the ravages of a bad economy.

☞ PASSION FOR ACTION.

James O'Toole, a leadership expert, says, "Ninety-five percent of American managers today say the right thing. Five percent actually do it." We need action-oriented leadership in organizations. Such leaders focus on performance, mission accomplishment and facilitation of change, not on philosophy and action-less talk.

The action-oriented leader can see the opportunities change brings. Innovative leaders make change happen even though it goes against established rules, regulations, and protocol. By capturing these opportunities, an organization becomes more flexible and competitive.

Lee Iaccoca is a man known for his actions. Several years into his tenure as President of Chrysler Motor Company, he had an intuition. He felt it was time to bring back the convertible. He went to his engineers and asked them how long it would take to put one on the street. The engineers estimated it would take three to five years to build the convertible. Ioccoca's impatience flared. He told them he couldn't wait that long. Orders came down to take a car off the assembly line and cut off the roof. Now, the prototype model was ready.

Iaccoca got into the car and drove it across town, doing his own marketing analysis. He counted the hands of the people who stopped and waved. Bold actions are required to overcome the rules and procedures that slow down businesses.

Dominoes Pizza Distribution increased its sales from $5 million to $600 million in just eight years. They did it by taking the right actions. In the 1980s, people from the field swamped the corporate offices with phone calls. Top management wondered why they were being called to clarify various policies and procedures. Why weren't people in the field making their own decisions?

After careful analysis, they found the reason. It was their policy manual. The manual had grown to 10 inches thick. A few of the managers flew to the Michigan commissary, found a container, and burned the manual in front of everyone. Shortly thereafter, all offices began destroying other policy manuals. Now the field had to make decisions on their own. There was no policy manual to hide behind. The phone calls quit coming in, and profits started going up.

A leader's actions must focus on removing barriers and obstacles that have developed through years of neglect and bureaucratic management. Typically, restrictive rules and regulations become barriers preventing people from doing what's right. Rules and regulations become obsolete and outdated but never seem to go away. Like ocean sediment, layer after layer builds up, becoming glue in the wheels of progress. Innovative leaders must have a healthy disrespect for barriers and obstacles. By taking a "proceed until apprehended" attitude, the removal of these obstacles and barriers will open doors of innovation and creativity. Bureaucracy never improves until an action-oriented leader courageously makes it happen.

☞ PASSION FOR PEOPLE.

General William Livsey once said, "You can assign a man to a leadership position but no one will ever really be a leader until his appointment is ratified in the hearts and minds of his soldiers." Leadership is earned. It is not based on titles, position, or rank. The business that neglects its people and treats them solely as expendable resources stands to incur a great loss. A people-oriented leader understands how, why, and what motivates people at work.

Far too many organizations have a bottom-line, short-term, mentality. Productivity largely has to do with a softer side of management. Bob Moawab, CEO of the Edge Learning Institute, says, "Most organizations help people become better employees. The best organizations help employees become better people." The innovative enterprise recognizes that people work for more reasons than just money.

I entered the Army a few months after graduating from college. As a Second Lieutenant, I was at the bottom of the hierarchy in the commissioned officer ranks. As with most officers just starting out, my book of experience was only about two pages long. I was confused, frustrated, and looked for someone to help me grow as a leader.

My company commander was a remarkable person. Joe came up through the ranks as a Special Forces medic in Vietnam. I enjoyed working for him because he was a caring leader. Not only did he take care of "his" Lieutenants, but he took care of all the men and women in the company.

Since I was one of newest officers in the battalion, I was obligated to "pull duty." Duty lasted 24 hours, and I was supposed to be "in charge" after everyone else went home for the day. The duty officer's manual said my responsibilities included providing security and ensuring our battalion was ready to go-to-war. What duty really meant was that I had to "baby sit" an entire battalion of about 600 soldiers.

As luck would have it, my turn fell on New Years Day, one of the worst days in the year to have duty. The day just went on and on. Halfway through the day, I got a call from Joe, my commander. He wanted to know if I had made any plans for lunch. He and his wife had cooked something, and he wanted to bring some lunch over to me. I didn't know what to say, except, "Sure!"

It was a meal I never forgot. This one small act of kindness did something special—it showed me he really cared. It taught me more about leadership than reading dozens of management books. There is an old saying in the military, "If you take care of your troops, your troops will take care of you." Through that one act, Joe gained a tremendous amount of respect and admiration. His leadership style was based on caring. Through caring for others, he accomplished a great deal.

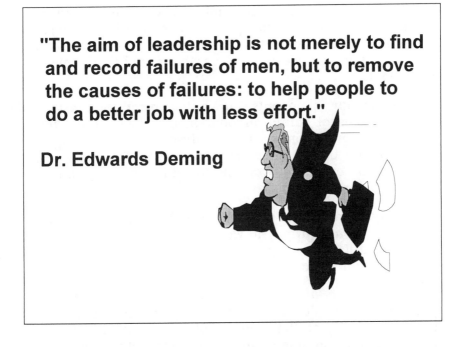

"The aim of leadership is not merely to find and record failures of men, but to remove the causes of failures: to help people to do a better job with less effort."

Dr. Edwards Deming

LEADERSHIP BEATITUDES

Today's business environment requires a whole new set of leadership characteristics. These characteristics provide the energy to make people want to change a bureaucratic environment into an innovative one. Uniquely equipped for this task is the innovative leader who possesses the "Leadership Beatitudes."

BE BOLD AND CHALLENGE STATUS QUO

"Leadership is the ability to get other people to do what they don't want, and like it," at least according to Harry Truman. Conformity and status quo are the first steps toward business ineffectiveness. People become comfortable doing the same things the same way, copying everyone else. Sad to say, but conformity and habit are sure ways leading to business failure.

Flying on Southwest Airlines quickly showed me that they are a nonconformist airline. Their product is exciting. Everything from the tickets and boarding passes to the casual dress and occasional costumes attendants wear give clear a clear indication something is different.

Occasionally, attendants sing or stage a rap song instead of reading the usual boring announcements other airlines make. Obviously, it must work because Southwest is the most profitable airline in the United States. Herb Kelleher, CEO and founder, combines fun and hard work into something he calls "management by fooling around."

One attendant stated why Southwest Airlines is successful. She said, "Herb is a great guy to work for. He knows all of our first names, and if I have a problem with the company, I can talk directly to him about it."

All managers at Southwest work at a job other than their primary jobs one day a quarter. They may work as a luggage handler, gate agent, flight attendant, or any other position, as long as it is a front-line position. This helps all managers learn more about the company. Even Herb has been seen loading luggage onto his planes.

Kelleher's nonconformist philosophy serves a major purpose. He wants his executives to be guiding examples. Herb feels everyone is a leader, and he empowers people to make decisions. It's been his intent to limit rules and regulations so that people can make decisions at the lowest possible level. As Herb says, "We tell our people that we value inconsistency."

The innovative leader is always looking for ways to improve what is being done, and is never satisfied with just being good. In today's chaotic business environment, good is no longer good enough.

BE A RISK TAKER

Christopher Columbus visualized his journey to the Far East. He had never been there before. The only information he possessed was what Marco Polo had written. So Columbus went to work. He organized and gathered the resources needed for his journey. He and his three ships sailed for thirty days at sea before they sighted land. He faced down a mutiny, and overcame a big risk while everyone else stayed safely on land. He went beyond the horizon and traveled further than any of the explorers at that time.

Leadership means becoming comfortable with ambiguity. Followers are willing to take risks and accept a challenging role if the leader sets the example. People want to be challenged, and they want leaders who are willing to go out on a limb. A challenging mission will bring out the best in people.

Leadership means you are in the front leading, not safely managing the rear. The innovative leader understands that progress depends on change and that change is risky. The leader creates an environment allowing people freedom to experiment and take risks without fear of reprisal. The innovative leader provides support and encouragement to his or her people even if a person fails in trying to do something new.

BE AUTHENTIC AND APPROACHABLE

The people you lead know you by observing your behavior, the way you talk to them, and your actions. Everyone asks themselves one question about the person they work for: "Is this person for real or are they a fake?" They honestly want to know if a leader is a phony or sincerely cares about them and the business?

One way to make yourself approachable is to talk openly about your own mistakes and your limitations. Once viewed as taboo and poor leadership, this approach is now more acceptable and no longer thought of as a sign of weakness. In fact, many people find it a sign of strength and authenticity, a way to gain respect and trust from your people. After all, who doesn't make mistakes—it's only human.

I was asked by a bank president to meet with his executive team to discuss how to make their bank more competitive. This bank had a successful thirty-year history and was one of the first banks built in the city.

Everyone, including the president, sat around a conference table. I asked them to tell me what they thought was working well and what they thought needed improving. Each member of the executive team expressed honest opinions of what they saw and felt. Some things they said were positive and complimentary. Other comments, just as easily discussed, were problematic areas needing correction. The communication was open and honest.

The reason they were comfortable discussing both the positive and negative aspects was due to the bank president. The president was very approachable and highly respected. In many hierarchical businesses one's career is on the line for bringing up problems. This was not true here. The president had created an environment where it was acceptable to openly express feelings and concerns about problems. Once problems are in the open, they can be solved taking the organization to the next performance level.

Terry Paulson, author of *They Shoot Managers Don't They*, tells the story about a CEO and a group of senior officers in a meeting. The CEO started the meeting by putting a $100 bill on the table. Then he began telling the group about the major mistake he had made messing up an important project. He then challenged each of his staff members to top the story with a story of their own. If they could, they could have the $100. What he did was fitting. He was saying it's all right to make mistakes and more importantly, it's all right to tell people about them, rather than cover them up. Creating an open environment by giving them an incentive to keep trying is important if you want your people to become innovative.

BE A ROLE MODEL

The old saying goes, "Actions speak louder than words." This saying is more true today than ever before. Change begins at the front office, the top floor, the corporate boardroom. Workers are not fooled by posters, slogans, and speeches such as, "People are our most important asset" or "Quality comes first." Management's actions show the people in the organization what is truly important. You must walk the talk.

People carry mental yardsticks measuring differences between what their leaders say and what they do. As we said previously, many management programs and philosophies fail to take root because the behavior of management doesn't change. The behavior and actions must begin at the front office.

I visited a hospital and was given a briefing on their new management philosophy. The briefer proudly told me all their employees were treated equally. "Everyone has the same rights as everyone else," he said. The briefing was impressive but when I left to go back to my hotel, I noticed the truth.

I saw the employees and patients had to cross a dangerous intersection and walk quite a distance to their cars, while the executive staff had reserved parking spaces closest to the hospital. Small things make major differences, and no one was fooled regarding how this hospital felt about equality.

BE OUT AND ABOUT

The world's greatest ideas didn't come out of committees or meetings. The best ideas and solutions to problems are found at the front line with the workers. The world's best ideas and opportunities are generated at the loading docks, in break rooms, and in the car to and from the office.

In this high-tech, fast-paced world, meetings and conferences become vampires slowly draining the life out of the business. Change occurs so rapidly that by the time a problem or opportunity is brought up in a staff meeting, it's too late to react effectively. Leaders must get out of the office and spend time talking to workers and customers about the business.

The best innovators are the workers because they know how to get the job done, and they know what prevents them from doing it. Leaders are busy people, and it is easy to allow the tyranny of the urgent to get in the way of the important.

Nothing is as powerful as the senior executive's presence outside the conference room. Just listening to people sends powerful messages to everyone in the organization. Talking is important too, but listening is better. Don't confuse talking to people with giving a prepared speech or giving orders—just talk to them. This shows that you care and provides opportunities to discover new ideas and find areas that need improvement. Walking the corridors and talking to people will do more for creating the kind of place you want than a hundred speeches and thousands of e-mail messages. Get out and talk to your people.

BE COURAGEOUS

Innovative leadership involves taking a direction that is different from everyone else's. It takes courage to take a stand contrary to what others are doing. The men and women of America are looking for a challenging opportunity to make a difference. People are quickly growing tired with political correctness. They are looking for courageous leaders to take a stand, ones who are unafraid to take them where they have never been before. Leadership is not based on popularity, but on action and passion.

Pratt & Whitney had a proud tradition of service building aircraft engines for decades. Thousands of Americans flew in combat bombers and fighters using the Pratt & Whitney engines. Several years ago United Technologies bought the Pratt & Whitney aircraft engine company. Living in Columbus, Georgia, at the time, I remember when United Technologies tried to replace the Pratt & Whitney sign at the front gate of the plant.

The community and hundreds of courageous workers raised a tremendous uproar. The emotion was so profound that United Technologies backed down, deciding to keep the original company sign. It may not have been politically correct, but these workers were both passionate and courageous about maintaining a proud tradition.

BE INSPIRATIONAL

Horst Shultze, the CEO of Ritz-Carlton Hotels, delivered one of the most inspiring and motivating talks I ever heard. The vision for his company unfolded like an artist painting a canvas.

He spoke of his dream of creating, not just good hotels, but the best hotel chain in the world. He recounted how his workers told him what the hotel industry needed, what was important, and how to do it. The audience seated in the auditorium became part of the transformation process. They felt the workers' pride and enthusiasm. They could see the difference this leader brought to his organization.

Throughout his talk, he kept the audience sitting on the edge of its seats. He did not read prepared text written by some speech writer, but he spoke from his heart. The difference in his talk and other "speeches" was that you could feel his commitment and caring attitude. It wasn't the words he used, but the tone of his words and his gestures that made the difference. He was passionate, inspiring, and planted a seed in all of us. It was clear to the audience that Mr. Horst Shultze possessed the "Beatitudes of Leadership."

The Leadership Beatitudes are:

→ **Be Bold and Challenge Status Quo**

→ **Be a Risk Taker**

→ **Be Authentic and Approachable**

→ **Be a Role Model**

→ **Be Out and About**

→ **Be Courageous**

→ **Be Inspirational**

Innovative Leadership

Assessment

A *leader* is **a person who inspires you to take a journey to a destination you would not go to by yourself.** The traditional manager who maintains the status quo the same way it was will not be effective in today's environment. Today's business challenges revolve around change, innovation, passion, and creativity. I developed the Innovative Leadership Self-Assessment Guide as a tool for those who want to know what competencies lead to business success now and in the future.

As times change, leadership skills must also change. What was successful in the past is still relevant, but may not be everything needed for the future. Use this assessment tool to rate yourself or your business. You can also give it to others and have them provide you with an honest appraisal.

INNOVATIVE LEADERSHIP SELF-ASSESSMENT GUIDE

Process Management. An innovative leader designs and manages processes that are efficient and effective. These processes support the delivery of either the organization's service or the manufacture of the organization's products. Processes move horizontally across organizational boundaries. Score yourself higher if you have identified your critical processes.

Customer Driven. One of the highest leadership priorities is the ability to focus on the needs and expectations of customers. Does the organization build and maintain relationships with customers? Does the enterprise have devices in place to measure customer satisfaction (customers can also be employees) and customer loyalty? Add points if you know the needs, expectations, and desires of your customers. Deduct points if there are only certain select parts of the organization having this information.

Information Management. The innovative enterprise thrives on information. There are multiple avenues and many ways to express the goals, plans, and status of the organization to all people working within the enterprise. The enterprise shares success stories and ideas with everyone. What means are available to improve communication (e.g., meetings, LANs, bulletin boards, E-mail, etc.)? Score yourself lower if there is no organized system in place to spread information.

Change Management. An innovative leader is knowledgeable of and manages change appropriately. Such a leader weaves ongoing programs and management philosophies into the strategic or business planning. Deduct points if your organizational structure has not flattened in the past four years. Deduct more points if your last change action created anger, resentment, and frustration.

Innovation. An innovative leader makes focused efforts to initiate new ideas and suggestions. The leader is constantly looking beyond the horizon at other industries and trends to see new ways to do things. The organization does not maintain status quo. Add one point if people from your organization have taken site visits or benchmarked other organizations during the past six months.

Continuous Improvement. An innovative leader is continuously improving everything the enterprise does. Processes and procedures are constantly being improved. Score yourself higher if you have a continuous improvement program. Deduct one point if it is only a "suggestion box."

Obstacle Removal. The innovative leader spends time identifying and removing barriers and obstacles obstructing work flow. Employees feel free to go to anyone in the organization for advice and assistance. Deduct points if you have not had an employee survey or sensing session during the past year.

☐ **Charts the Course.** An innovative leader provides a clear direction toward the future. Is the leader inspiring others to take a journey to a particular destination? If there is no clear direction or inspiring vision, mark yourself low. Give yourself points if many people are involved in the goal-setting process.

☐ **Provides Motivation.** An innovative leader provides a system of reward and recognition. Team-based rewards lead to higher morale. Employees should feel that they are contributing to the vitality of the enterprise. Give yourself two points if you have provided recognition to a worker or team during the past five days. Reduce points if you only recognize length of service.

☐ **Creates Trust Building**. An innovative leader allows people to learn from their mistakes and allows risk taking. The leader who tolerates risk taking scores higher in innovation. Bad signs are more than two signatures required on any form, and too many auditors, inspectors, and time clocks.

☐ **Provides Purpose.** Purpose gives people a reason why they should work for this organization. People relate best to the enterprise when they understand how their actions relate to the big picture. The person who understands how their actions affect the organization is more empowered to take action.

TOTAL

SCORE

Scoring Directions. Rate yourself or your organization on a scale of 1 (lowest) to 5 (highest) for each item. This assessment can be also be used by others to rate your standing in the organization.

Rating the results:

Excellent	**55–50**
Good	**49–44**
Average	**43–33**
Needs Improvement	**32–0**

CHAPTER 6

Barriers to Innovation and Creativity

"Regulations are for the wise men to follow wisely and for fools to follow blindly."

—BG James Turner,
USAF, 482nd Fighter Wing

Organizations have unintentionally created many barriers and obstacles to innovation and creativity. All business leaders must take deliberate actions to remove these barriers and obstacles. This, above all other responsibilities, must be one of the innovative leader's top priorities. This is not easy and requires continuous effort, endurance, and courageous action on the part of the leader.

The innovative leader improves performance by looking at what is done and how well it is done. Improving performance is the result of removing barriers and obstacles that interfere with people who are doing their job. This means it's management's job to identify and do the right things, and eliminate the wrong things.

Many businesses and organizations encounter resistance to change and to new ideas. This resistance to change is often a self-protecting mechanism. Over the years bureaucratic rules have been put in place to protect jobs and functions that are no longer essential. Some barriers were created because someone made a mistake twenty years ago, and now there is a rule affecting everyone. The cumulative effect eats up valuable resources, robs pride of ownership and initiative, and prevents people from doing what is right. It becomes nonstop warfare.

Removing Barriers and Obstacles

The pointman on a military patrol performs a valuable function. The pointman walks far ahead of the formation clearing the way for the rest of the soldiers following closely behind. By checking for and removing enemy mines, ambushes, and obstacles impeding the progress of the main body, the pointman insures the group moves safely and quickly. Once the obstacles are removed, the patrol moves safely through, reaching their destination. The pointman remains the most valuable, as well as the most vulnerable, person in the organization.

Just like the pointman, the innovative leader must swing into high gear. The leader clears paths for innovation by painstakingly devoting time combating obsolete and overly restrictive policies

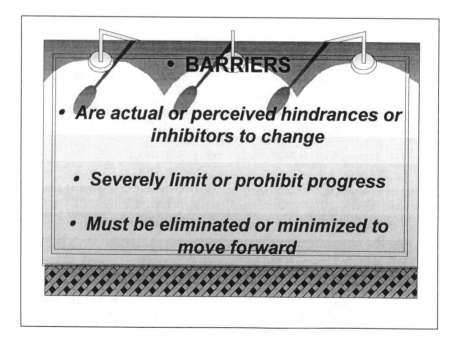

- **BARRIERS**
- *Are actual or perceived hindrances or inhibitors to change*
- *Severely limit or prohibit progress*
- *Must be eliminated or minimized to move forward*

and procedures. Innovative leaders should focus on the strategies outlined below when removing barriers and obstacles to innovation and creativity:

→ Removing barriers that rob people of pride of ownership.

→ Removing barriers that keep people from reaching their potential.

→ Removing barriers that inhibit trust.

→ Removing barriers that prevent exceptional customer service.

→ Removing barriers that prevent people from doing the right thing.

Often managers don't see the entire picture. What may appear as a small problem to management is a major obstacle affecting the front-line worker. The problems increase in magnification at the bottom of the organizational pyramid.

There are many businesses and organizations leading the way, doing what is right. I discuss this in Chapter 3. Ritz-Carlton Hotels has built the best hotels in the world by removing defects in everything they do. Police Chief Greenburg from Charleston, South Carolina, has pushed back crime to the same levels as thirty years ago. Then there is Wainwright Industries, who created a work environment of trust, equality, and customer service. The leaders of these organizations realized the secret of success is no secret. By removing barriers and obstacles impacting on the front-line, success becomes much more obtainable.

Continuously Improving by Removing Defects

Managers mean well, but occasionally they go about management in the wrong way. How many times have you heard your boss say, "Don't bring me a problem unless you bring a solution"? What if the solution to the problem is beyond your control? Isn't the identification process half the solution? When faced with this

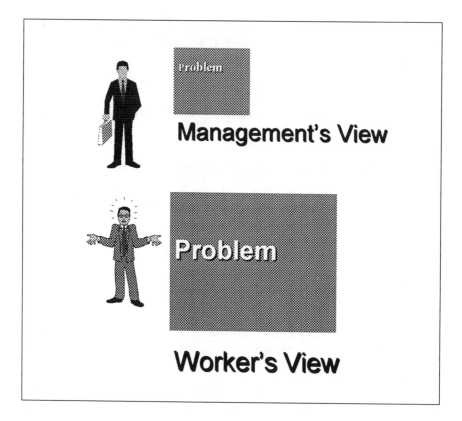

dilemma of bringing the solution, most workers may take the path of least resistance. They will look the other way and ignore the problem. Unfortunately, the problem will not go away, but will continue to fester, creating a much larger problem later.

The boss's job is to remove the barriers and obstacles, thus helping people do a better job. Problems brought to management's attention usually show they are beyond the workers' control. Most workers are unable to fix the problem themselves. It requires a higher authority or a collaborative effort between groups of people.

Ritz-Carlton Hotels does many things well. I am particularly impressed by the process they use to remove defects, continuously improving everything they do. Maybe that is why they have been voted as the best hotel in the world for many years running.

At these world class hotels, fixing problems and improving service doesn't happen accidentally. They have created an ongoing, daily process of focusing on all the major aspects of the hotel. Guests who stay at the hotel several times receive special treatment. If a guest wants a cold soft drink available in the room upon arrival, there is a defect-free process to insure it. The right soft drink, at the right temperature, is delivered to the room at the right time. Understand that the characteristic "right" is specified by the guest, and is not based on a whim or staff convenience. If a guest requests a goose down pillow instead of a synthetic pillow, it will be in the room before the guest checks in, not thirty minutes later. The hotels have a computer network linking all this data with each hotel worldwide.

The hotel chain is moving toward the Self-Directed Work Team concept. A team of housekeeping personnel at the Ritz-Carlton in Dearborn, Massachusetts, streamlined the housekeeping cycle time. They changed from one person cleaning each room to two people. By designing the specific steps and tools needed to clean rooms, the cleaning process became more efficient and quicker. Workers asked for and got special knee pads to reduce discomfort when cleaning bathrooms. Now they get all the rooms cleaned in half the time and also saved $458,000.

In Atlanta, guests were getting telephone busy signals when trying to make reservations. Once the problem was noted, the Reservations Department added another person just to catch the overflow. A corner mirror added to an employee hallway avoided accidental collisions and prevented employees from getting injured.

How does the Ritz-Carlton do this? As Yogi Berra once said, "It all starts at the beginning." All Ritz-Carlton employees attend a comprehensive employee orientation process. Among other things, employees learn about the Internal Defect Form (IDF). Any employee noticing a deficiency or defect during the normal work day writes an IDF. Once collected, the forms are forwarded to the hotel Quality Office for consolidation. The Quality Office tracks them and sends them to the appropriate department for action. Department managers and Quality Coaches take action to either repair or replace the defect, or tell the department staff of the problem.

Each department in each hotel worldwide has a "Stand-up." Perhaps similar to a military inspection, each shift, all employees receive a 15–20 minute class on the same topic across the globe. "Stand-ups" provide information and training for the staff each day. Whether it is the Ritz-Carlton in Naples, Italy, or in Buckhead, Atlanta, everyone gets the same class. The shift leader inspects each person, insuring proper uniform, nametag, and appearance. Stand-ups may include questions about one of Ritz-Carlton's twenty basics. Finally, announcements are made, guest preferences are discussed, and the shift begins this way—each shift, each day, each hotel, around the world.

Ritz-Carlton is in a nonstop race to eliminate all defects. In 1992, 30 percent of their customers experienced a defect during their stay. In 1995, only 6.4 percent of their customers experience defects. Doing it right the first time is more than just a philosophical discussion. Mr. Shulzte, the CEO, points out that in 1994 sales increased by $75 million using 500,000 fewer labor-hours. It was accomplished by eliminating defects, rework, and unnecessary steps in key processes.

Vampire Functions: Doing Wrong Things Right

You may be wondering, "How can I be innovative when I'm up to my elbows with alligators? Who can be innovative when every day is a struggle when facing fewer dollars and fewer people?" Stop to think for a moment. Isn't this the best time to become innovative?

Albert Einstein said, "The important thing is not to stop questioning." That sentiment applies to many facets of life—science, relationships, philosophy, and education. This is particularly important with today's management methods.

Work consists of various tasks and functions. Functions come in two basic types. There are those that add value and those that do not add value, i.e., non-value added and value-added functions. Business is about doing the value-added tasks and functions. Any function that doesn't add value to the business is what I call a "vampire function."

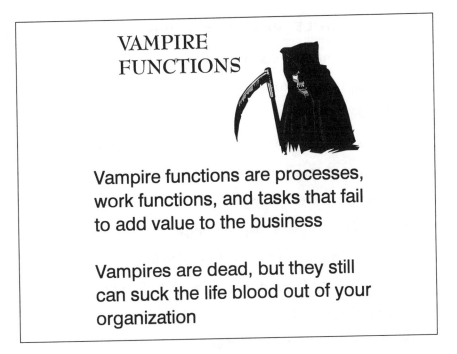

VAMPIRE FUNCTIONS

Vampire functions are processes, work functions, and tasks that fail to add value to the business

Vampires are dead, but they still can suck the life blood out of your organization

These vampire functions consume precious resources and have little positive influence on anything important. A tremendous amount of time and resources go into doing the wrong things. My experience shows traditional organizations expend anywhere from 20 to 40 percent of their time, effort, and resources doing unnecessary or duplicated work. There are entire departments performing functions that are no longer adding value and are no longer needed.

A vampire has one main function—to drink blood. The only good vampire is a dead vampire. Even when vampires are dead, they still have the capacity to drain the life out of you or your organization.

In this case, innovation simply means deciding what the organization should eliminate, streamline, or just quit doing all together. Ask yourself, "Is that report we have filled out for forty years still necessary? Do all those policies and procedures still make sense?" Continually question what you are doing and what your organization is doing. Regularly question the procedures and approaches, i.e., think innovation.

SAMPLE VAMPIRE FUNCTIONS

→ Unnecessary reports and administrative requirements

→ Administrative costs and overhead

→ Waste and rework

→ Steps and tasks not adding value to the process

→ Doing too many audits and inspections

→ Doing the wrong things right

→ Too many unnecessary meetings

→ Counting things that don't need counting

→ Unnecessary forms and paperwork to fill out

→ Overly restrictive rules and regulations

→ Overplanning for every event

Eliminating Vampire Functions improves:

→ Productivity

→ Effectiveness

→ The bottom line

→ Timely response to customers

Doing the Right Things Right improves:

→ Morale of the workforce

→ Customer satisfaction

→ Respect and caring within the workforce

→ Positive attitudes toward management

Vampire Extermination Expeditions

Vampires have to be exterminated. Television and fictional video shows the holly stake and the silver bullet as the only effective tools against vampires. By adding an entertaining approach, work can become fun, entertaining, and productive. I've developed a unique work session called "vampire extermination expeditions." During the expedition, we take representatives from the organization and search out, identify, and exterminate non-value added vampire functions. These sessions can last from one to three days. The result of these expeditions frees the organization from the troublesome barnacles slowing the organization down.

You must decide to fix your problems or ignore your problems. Which is cheaper? The process of innovation is a science. Improvement comes from a systematic approach of identifying and eliminating barriers, problems, and obstacles.

Summary

→ Management's view of problems is only the tip of the iceberg.

→ It is management's job to remove barriers and obstacles.

→ Managers must develop processes to identify and eliminate barriers and obstacles.

→ Tremendous improvement comes from small changes.

Red Tape and Unnecessary Paperwork

Each year businesses generate 2.5 trillion pieces of paper. One-third of those are forms. Corporations spend $100 billion each year in processing forms. Excessive paperwork is driving healthcare expenses higher. Estimates show the cost of claim forms in the healthcare industry alone is $40 billion a year. There are over 450 different claim forms for a total of four billion claims. Doctor's and medical offices spend 17 hours a week on administrative duties.

"I can't stand the proliferation of paperwork. It's useless to fight the forms. You've got to kill the people producing them."

Vladimir Kabaidze
USSR

Whether it is filling out forms, lab slips, or claim forms, most of administrative tasks are done on paper.

Approximately 25–35 percent of the people working in insurance companies do nothing more than process paper. Blue Cross-Blue Shield gets 20 million pieces of paper in the mail every year. It takes 25 clerks to open, sort, and forward the paperwork to the proper departments.

To help reduce their paperwork problem, in 1990 IBM initiated its "Solution Central." Solution Central is a special service desk for the sole purpose of helping employees overcome the in-house bureaucracy. There are 50 people on call 95 hours a week and on weekends to help overcome bureaucracy. Probably the most drastic approach to eliminating paperwork was illustrated by Vladimir Kabaidze of the former U.S.S.R. He said, "I can't stand the proliferation of paperwork. It's useless to fight the forms. You've got to kill the people producing them."

> ## "Regulations are for wise men to follow wisely and for fools to follow blindly."
>
> -BG James Turner
> 482nd Fighter Wing

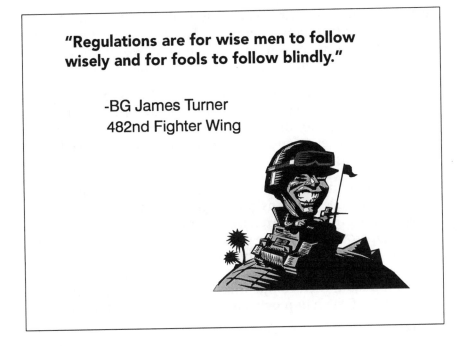

Proceed Until Apprehended

The Mayor of Los Angeles, Richard Riordan, learned quickly how to work within a bureaucracy. Riordan had worked in the civilian sector for many years and was unafraid to challenge the status quo. He wanted to remove an unnecessary tow-away zone on a public street in the garment district. But first he had to challenge a 25-page memorandum outlining various permissions, rules and regulations, hearings, and other hurdles to jump before the tow-away zone could be removed. His impatience and frustration with the bureaucratic system motivated others to action. So one night, one of his officials and his son took their car and removed all the signs. They decided, "if you can't work with the system, go around it."

Trust Building: The Foundation for Innovation

Building trust between workers and management is another important element in building the innovative enterprise. In the

1970s and the 1980s, American auto makers were fighting fierce competition with Japanese imports. The auto industry was in a state of chaos. Like molten lava, the chaos flowed downhill to all auto parts manufacturers, including Wainwright Industries.

Wainwright Industries is located in St. Peters, Missouri, and was a 1994 National Malcolm Baldrige Quality Award (NMBQA) winner (see Appendix B). They have 275 associates and $30 million in sales. They manufacture parts for the automobile and aerospace industry.

Wainwright discovered the way they were manufacturing parts in the 70s and 80s wasn't as good as it needed to be. They were no longer competitive. Facing a recession, sales dropped from $5 to $3 million. Operations slowed to three days a week, and tensions grew between employees and management. The environment was not productive and would not lead to the innovative environment they needed to regain their competitiveness. So they started changing. They focused first on improving internal communication and trust.

The first step was to start calling the workers, "associates." This one small change lead to even more significant changes. They threw away the time clocks, and everyone was put on a salary. Today, associates are paid even if they miss work and paid time-and-a-half for overtime. Trust between worker and management took a giant leap forward.

Next came the uniforms. No more ties and white shirts for managers and blue shirts for the workers. Everyone in the organization now wears a uniform, including the chairman and the professional staff. The uniform consists of a pair of black slacks and a white pinstripe shirt. On the shirt each person has his or her name emblazoned on one side, and the other side has "Team Wainwright." Of course, not everyone liked the idea at first. Now everyone accepts it and feels it is more practical. It created a greater feeling of equality.

A team of associates developed a profit-sharing program for everyone at Wainwright. The team consisted of one manager and seven non-management associates. Ownership developed, propelling them down the track at a faster pace. Yes, even the books are open for everyone to see. No secrets—everyone has access to the financial records.

As in most industries, training remains the discriminator between average businesses and those who are exceptional. Wainwright's emphasis on training created "employability security" within each associate. Even when the economy dips and work slows down, Wainwright does not automatically lay off workers. They attempt to reassign as many of them as possible—no promises made. If they have to let someone go, they have at least provided them with training and skills, making them more employable for other jobs or in another industry.

The feeling of trust and equality they have created has paid back in many results. Attendance records show the proof. Except in 1994, when attendance dipped to 98.9 percent, since 1984 attendance has consistently averaged 99 percent. Not only is there an increased feeling of trust, equality, and ownership, but profits have grown from $5 million to $30 million.

Rewarding Mistakes

Many people talk about trust and equality, but when something goes wrong or when an accident occurs—look out. I remember all too often how the hammer falls looking to find a person to blame. You cannot say you trust people only then to punish them when an accident occurs.

Most accidents are not caused by people, but by situations out of the individual's control. Does this mean you tolerate accident-prone situations? Of course not. You have to discriminate between negligence or a situation out of the individual's control. Was it preventable and was the person trying to do the right thing?

Wainwright recognized several facts. If you want people to learn, if you want innovative ideas, if you want people to fix problems, you can't punish them for accidents. Most accidents are not people problems, but system problems.

Wainwright Industries has a plant in Texas where they were trying to instill this new culture of trust and equality. Workers were accidentally damaging doors with their forklifts and other mechanical equipment. The culture at that time was restrictive and fearful. The workers were afraid to report accidents because they thought they would get fired.

One day, one brave soul took a chance and admitted his accident to the chief operating officer. He had just damaged an overhead door when he was moving some racks. The CEO called a plant-wide meeting and explained to everyone what happened. Silence—they waited for the shoe to fall. The CEO called the man up and shook his hand in front of everyone. Lesson learned. Overnight, people started reporting accidents. Accident reporting went from 0 percent to 90 percent. They eliminated the specter of fear, guilt, and punishment. Now, they can openly identify, fix, and repair defects and other accidents eating at the bottom line. Here are a few other ways to help build trust.

Do:

→ **Look out for people and their best interests.**

→ **Treat people with dignity.**

→ **Show confidence in their ability.**

→ **Listen carefully to what people are saying.**

→ **Deliver on the promises you make.**

→ **Be authentic and share yourself openly.**

→ **Feel free to admit your own mistakes.**

→ **Include others in decision-making processes.**

→ **Always tell the truth.**

Don't:

→ **Jump to conclusions before you have the facts.**

→ **Blame people for problems they have no control over.**

→ **Hold back information, including bad news.**

→ **Avoid taking responsibility.**

→ **Feel like you have to have all the answers.**

→ **Make excuses when it doesn't work the way you wanted.**

→ **Be a perfectionist.**

Doing Right Things Right—Solving Crime Using Common Sense

Police departments across the United States are falling into the black hole of bureaucracy. They hire more and more police officers and buy more and more equipment with the following results— more and more crime. On the other hand, Chief Ruben Greenburg, Police Chief of Charleston, South Carolina, has an innovative way of keeping crime off the streets. He uses common sense and has generated an impressive lineup of statistics. In 1994 there were:

☺ No fatalities and only four robberies occurred in public housing areas.

☺ No one was paroled for robbery, burglary, or sexual assault.

☺ No juvenile fatalities occurred during the past five years.

☺ No school kids were shot or stabbed during school days.

☺ The lowest number of homicides in the past 30 years were recorded.

☺ The lowest number of robberies and burglaries in the past 30 years were recorded.

☺ Domestic violence decreased.

☺ Drug related crimes decreased.

Remarkable as it seems, these accomplishments occurred with no additional staff, no additional money, and no new laws. While all this was going on, Charleston experienced a 50 percent growth in it's population. Seems too good to be true? It is true, and the TV show "60 Minutes" went to Charleston and verified the facts.

Drug-Related Crimes

Dealing drugs is an incestuous affair. Like termites on a wooden structure, small drug dealers infiltrate the city landscape and start destroying legitimate community and business life. Customers, families, and other legitimate businesses dry up, leaving the area. Places that once flourished with city parks and trees look like the moon's surface, scared and barren. Charleston was no different. Drug dealing moved into the city, and crime rates rocketed.

Police officials analyzed the problem and discovered how to disrupt the drug-dealing cycle of events. Discovery came in accidentally from the drug dealers themselves. The drug dealers came to the police and told them what was going on. The police noticed two important activities associated with drug dealing.

The first was how drug dealing attracted other criminal activities. Drug dealing took place in specific parts of the city. Drug dealing not only attracted drug buyers, but also robbers, thieves, and carjackers who preyed on the drug dealer's "customers." Most drug buyers carried cash so they made perfect targets. The "customers" drove into town to buy drugs. They themselves would be robbed and occasionally had their cars hijacked. Most of these "customers" did not report the crime because they didn't want people to know the reason they were in "that" part of town. These other related criminal activities usually went unreported and unnoticed by most people.

Because of the other crimes, the drug-dealing business was dropping off. The drug dealers started complaining and wanted the police to solve this problem. It was the drug dealers themselves who reported the robberies and carjackings to the police. That is how the police first discovered how this "business" operated.

The second activity they discovered was that the drug-dealing "business" operated within a predictable cycle of events. Greenburg says, "You must understand it before you can stop it." Charleston police decided the best way to stop drug dealing was to apply their resources surgically.

Instead of pouring in seven days-a-week, round-the-clock police surveillance, Greenburg had both cheaper and more innovative solutions. Drug dealing occurred most often between the hours of 6:00 P.M. and 2:00 A.M. Thursday, Friday, and Saturday. Goldberg's strategy concentrated on knocking down the drug trade by at least 30 percent. Most drug dealers deal in $5, $10 and $15 transactions. Losing 30 percent of their business would cripple them and that is exactly what happened. Drug dealing slowed to a trickle and that part of town sprang back to life.

Public Housing—Safest Housing in Town

Today in Charleston, public housing is the safest place to live in the city. Your chances of safety are highest in these areas versus the higher priced neighborhoods. It is the only place in town where cabbies and pizza deliverers feel safe. Greenburg applies common sense management to this situation, too.

Charleston runs public housing like other people run exclusive apartment complexes. The city set the admission guidelines. Applying a law that has been on the books for decades, the city decides who can live there and who can't. Common sense dictates, keeping those people out who commit crimes will result in less crime.

The guidelines had the following qualifications. Applicants had to be free of convictions from 11 types of crimes during the past 10 years. The list of crimes include child molesting, arson, and rape, etc. There are 10,000 people who live in public housing. In 1994, there were only four robberies and no homicides. In fact, crime rates are significantly higher in private homes and communities other than in Charleston's public housing areas.

Charleston's public housing now provides a safe and secure haven for economically disadvantaged people. Greenburg says, "These 'poor' people now have the same dreams and hopes as 'rich' people."

Problems with Parole

Communities that have parolees have higher crime rates. Greenburg reports 86 percent of burglars who are released on parole are rearrested within three years. One burglar, on the average, is usually responsible for 60–70 burglaries in a community. As you can see, it becomes quite expensive rearresting and processing criminals only to have them released to repeat the crimes again. Police officers have become tired and frustrated from this sickening cycle.

Charleston's innovative solution took on the parole system. Greenburg created a special department of three or four people targeting three crimes—burglary, robbery, and sexual assault. The department set goals to stop all paroles in these offenses—no exceptions. When a prisoner comes up for parole, a member of this special department attends the parole board meeting.

Members of the parole board now hear both sides of the story. They take the arrest photos of the prisoner and sometimes take the victim to the hearing. In most parole hearings across America, victims get little representation. Rarely does anyone represent the victim or the family. Years go by, and the emotion surrounding the crime fades away. The potential parolee puts on a business suit, gets a haircut, and you figure the rest. Police officials take a more punitive approach. They feel it is safer for the community to keep prisoners off the street and in prison.

In 1994, no one was paroled for these three offenses. In return, crime has returned to the same low rates of 30 years ago. The city has saved money by not having to recapture, rearrest, and retry criminals who have been released on parole.

Domestic Violence

Domestic violence presents a frustrating and dangerous situation for both the victim and the police. Police departments may tell you there is not much they can do to prevent or stop domestic violence. Recent events in America remind us of the tragedy associated with this issue that tears at all of our hearts. Again, Charleston took direct action reducing the tragedies related to domestic violence.

In recent years, Charleston has enjoyed a reduction in domestic violence. By applying swift action, officials have stopped fatalities in domestic incidents. They did this by identifying the patterns associated with spousal abuse. Once the patterns were identified, they carried out procedures to prevent its recurrence. Those procedures were:

→ Treat it as a crime. Make no distinction from any other crime. Just because the people have the same last names does not make it any less of a crime.

→ Automatic arrest. In all cases the perpetrator is arrested. Couples are not just told to work it out and call if they need help again. The person is taken to jail— no exceptions.

→ Location of the arrest. They've learned that where the perpetrator is arrested is a strong deterrent in preventing the crime from recurring again. Being arrested in front of one's peers, associates, and customers has a significant preventive impact. Greenburg relates a story about a well-respected, professional who was abusing his wife. The police went into his office, arrested him, made him stand spread-eagled, handcuffed him, and took him to jail. The crime didn't happen again.

→ Isolate the victim. The victim is immediately moved to a safe haven. If the victim wants to go to a relative's house in another state, the police department provides transportation at no cost to the person. The couple remains separated until the case goes to court.

Juvenile Crimes

One of the most alarming elements in society today is the rise of juvenile crimes and juvenile violence. Plaguing the juvenile justice system is a revolving door. Chief Greenburg is quick to point out, and all of us can echo, that there are no consequences for their negative behavior. The many stories of juveniles arrested 10, 20, and 30 times but never spend a day in jail are all too common.

Again, the city of Charleston was undaunted. Instead of spending scarce resources to catch and punish bad behavior, they took proactive measure to prevent juvenile crime. They used an "old" but nonetheless, innovative two-prong approach.

The first step included the strict enforcement of another old law that has been on the books for decades. The law said that school-age kids had to be either one of two places—at home or at school. The second step was they brought back to life the role of the venerable truant officer.

The truant officers work directly for the police department. Their sole purpose was to enforce the law and pick up all school-age kids not at school or at home. Kids are immediately apprehended and returned to school.

Any kid not in school stands out like a sore thumb. The enforcement of this law makes it really easy to pinpoint violators. If kids are hanging out in the mall, a phone call to the police department is all it takes. Regular police officers don't have to stop what they are doing to chase kids. Now they just call the truant officers, and the truant officers come and pick them up.

Teenagers driving cars when they should be in school are stopped, and the car is towed. Their parents must pay $45 to get the car back. Most parents only have to pay once to get the message. This program works nine months a year, and the police have their hands full during the summer.

Gun Stoppers Program

Three Charleston businesses donated $10,000. Now any person who spots another person with a gun can call the police department and report it. Police immediately take the description and investigate, and if need be, arrest the person with the gun. The person who reports the weapon receives $100 the same day.

For those of you who think Charleston is a militaristic environment, visit there and ask one of their 105,000 residents what they think. The statistics speak for themselves. The city has reduced crime and violence to levels 30 years ago. They've done it by enforcing laws that have been on the books for years. What is amazing is that they did it without creating a huge expensive bureaucracy. They did it without increasing the budget and did it without adding additional staff and police officers. Whose city streets would you rather walk down, yours or theirs?

Innovative Actions for Today's Businesses

What have you done differently in your business this year? What changes have you made lately? Are you still operating using the same management policies and techniques handed down prior to the Industrial Revolution? Well, it may be time to breathe new life into your organization. If you haven't realized it yet, the world has changed. People have changed, and the entire business fabric is under reconstruction.

Here are a few suggestions on how to energize your organization into a more innovative and customer-focused enterprise.

→ **Put managers and staff into the field to work with front-line workers several days each year.**

→ **Reduce regulations and policies by 50 percent. Paint a mailbox red and centrally locate it so people can deposit all dumb rules and regulations needing revision or elimination.**

→ Form a team to evaluate each nomination. Celebrate with a bonfire burning all the policies and procedures no longer needed.

→ If you haven't already, start a system of education and training for everyone in the business.

→ Practice true equality and eliminate all reserved parking spaces except those for the disabled.

→ Ask your workers frequently, "What can I do to make your job better, easier, or more productive?" Then do it.

→ Conduct frequent, unannounced recognition/award celebrations for workers.

→ Give employees permission to disagree with management.

→ Consider going beyond having the "Best Employee of the Month/Year" and recognize individuals and teams for different and innovative reasons.

→ Capture the creativity of people and have contests for the best idea of the month.

→ Start new ways to evaluate performance by allowing subordinates to evaluate their superiors through team evaluations or a 360-degree evaluation.

→ Eliminate altogether or flatten organization charts.

→ Reengineer most of your inspectors and auditors. Give them new responsibilities, such as internal consultants, customer service representatives, helpers, or instructors.

CHAPTER 7

Providing Direction and Managing Information

"The great thing in this world is not so much where we stand, as in what direction we are moving."
—Oliver Wendell Holmes

The HMS Rhoan was the most technologically advanced ship in the late 1800s. Now it rests 100 feet down on the bottom of the Atlantic ocean. It lies in mute testimony of a ship that lost it's course and was ravaged by a hurricane, sinking to an early grave. In the 1800s, shipwrecks were a common occurrence. But this was no ordinary ship nor were these an ordinary set of circumstances.

My wife and I lived in San Juan, Puerto Rico, for several years. We both learned how to scuba dive. After building our diving skills, we chartered a boat and went to the island of Tortola, one of the British Virgin Islands not too far from St. Thomas. We donned our scuba equipment and both of us sank to the bottom of the Atlantic. Although the wreck had been on the ocean bottom for almost 100 years, it was well preserved. We felt as if we were not alone, as if there was another presence around us.

My curiosity aroused, I immediately began research about what happened to this ship. Once back on the island of Tortola, I began my search. My research uncovered the disturbing facts surrounding the wreck of the Rhoan.

The HMS Rhoan was one of the modern ships of its time. It was one of the first steel-hulled steam ships and carried a crew of 135 of the best trained men available to the Royal Navy. It left Great Britain on a journey bound to Tortola with mail and supplies. But along the way it met its misfortune.

The clear skies and blue waters turned stormy. The storm turned into a hurricane, and the reef surrounding the island clenched its teeth. Suddenly, the weather turned the sea into a boiling cauldron. The Rhoan steamed off the coast of Tortola. As it came around the island, the hurricane appeared heading directly for the ship. Panic followed, rain bared down like steel bullets, and waves rose over the sides of the ship. For some reason, the ship turned away from the storm and tried to run away from the hurricane.

The ship was now without bearings or rudder, and chaos reigned. The waves finally conquered all remaining resistance, taking the ship down to the bottom of the ocean. On that day 125 of the 135 men on board perished.

Why did this ship sink? The least experienced sailor knows the answer. In a storm, ships must head into the storm, into the wind, not turn away. It is far safer to head into the storm than to try to turn away. The captain made the wrong decision, a fatal choice.

Businesses Need a New Vision

The parallel to business should be obvious. Today's business environment is not too unlike the hurricane the Rhoan faced. Companies that think they are sailing in calm seas today are only experiencing the calm before the storm. The Bible says, "Without a vision the people will perish." That is why establishing a direction—a vision—is so important. It keeps you heading in the right direction, from wrecking on the reef.

Walt Disney's vision was to "create the finest in family entertainment." A vision is a destination, the goal leading to the winning point. Winning at tennis involves landing the ball between the lines. A running back on a foot ball team must carry the ball over the goal lines. The quarterback, the ship's captain, the CEO, and the owner of the small business are responsible for choosing the right strategy for the right times, charting the right course.

Turning the Ship Around—Change Management

The role of the leader takes a new dimension. It takes time, training, and concentrated effort to change from an old way to a new way of doing business. Sometimes, it may take years before reaching a total transformation. It all begins with a vision for the future.

Brigadier General Warren Todd was the Commander of DeWitt Army Community Hospital at Fort Belvoir, Virginia, just outside Washington, DC. His vision for his hospital helped to create a striking difference between this hospital and others.

Beginning in May 1992, Brigadier General Todd lead a quality revolution. He took the traditional way of doing business and threw it out the door. He went beyond the usual superficial changes, building on new bedrock, focusing on high-end payoffs. He opened evening clinics, closed unneeded wards, consolidated outpatient clinics, and undertook a major training effort based on improving customer service and productivity.

In the past, the hospital had had a haphazard system managing pre-admissions. It was hit and miss, time consuming, and frustrating to the entire surgical staff. Several times, staff discovered missing EKGs, X-rays, and lab reports up to one hour prior to surgery.

A cross-functional team solved the administrative aspects surrounding surgical pre-admissions. DeWitt now has a one-stop, quick and easy pre-admission service completely reengineered by a team of physicians and nurses, and administrative and ancillary personnel.

Organization-wide training in any hospital is important. Training is even more critical when quality customer service is the goal. Here again, DeWitt was on target with its training efforts. They first began by picking 12 staff members to become internal facilitators. Each person received 4–5 weeks of train-the-trainer training. In turn, the 12 people cascaded training down to 40 other people. Now each department and service has access to a trained facilitator.

The facilitator serves as a team leader and became a coach, helping their individual departments reduce non-value added work. They also helped each department improve quality and customer service. DeWitt's example is one of the best ways to implement quality customer service.

Another team tackled the problematic process of education and training. Like many hospitals, responsibility for education and training is split among various hospital offices and departments. Here, three different offices controlled the hospital's conference rooms and classrooms. The team simplified the process by merging the three departments into one.

They came up with a new name for the training department. They call it "HEAT," or Hospital Education and Training. Now HEAT centrally manages all conference rooms and classrooms, hospital-wide training, and the training calendars for the entire hospital—a one-stop service. The project generated a new saying among hospital staff members. The saying is, "If you want training, you must go see someone in HEAT."

Probably the most significant result from all their efforts is improved patient satisfaction. For years, their Patient Representative Office tracked the number of complaints received versus the number of compliments they received. In 1992, their ratio was one-and-a-half complaints for every compliment. In 1993, they had one compliment for every complaint. In 1994, they were running two compliments for every one complaint.

Brigadier General Todd is quick to add that it hasn't been easy. At first, he spent an additional 30 percent more time communicating to his staff, an additional 4–5 hours a week. He remembers speaking every day for a week, on every shift, about quality and his vision for the hospital. DeWitt's vision statement is, "We will be the finest primary care center in Northern Virginia." He half jokingly adds, "I must have made that statement a billion times."

As the result of DeWitt's changes, he says his professional life is much more rewarding and tremendously more productive. No longer does he have to micro-manage decisions and every other aspect of the job. Looking back over the years, he confirms the fact that nothing would have changed without top leadership involvement. "It is just too easy to slip back in the old way of doing things," he said.

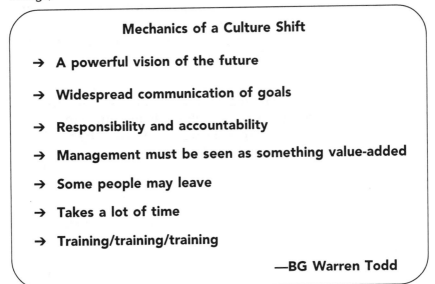

Mechanics of a Culture Shift

→ **A powerful vision of the future**

→ **Widespread communication of goals**

→ **Responsibility and accountability**

→ **Management must be seen as something value-added**

→ **Some people may leave**

→ **Takes a lot of time**

→ **Training/training/training**

—BG Warren Todd

Keeping the Ship on Course—Creating the Vision

The new leader is different from most people. Leaders have the responsibility to guide and to keep the organization on course, moving toward the destination it has chosen. The leader must see the connection between today and tomorrow and should be the catalyst for change. Consider the following story from the book, *Jurassic Park.*

In truth, neither Wu nor Arnold had the most important characteristic, Hammond decided. The Characteristic of vision. That great sweeping act of imagination which evoked a marvelous park, where children rested against the fences, wondering at the extraordinary creatures who come alive from their storybooks. Real vision. The ability to see the future. The ability to marshall resources to make that future vision a reality. No, neither Wu nor Arnold was suited for the task.

There are major differences between visionaries and leaders. The leader has to be more than just a visionary. Innovative leaders are both architects and builders. Leaders show how to create the vision as well as provide the leadership mobilizing others to reach it. On the other hand, the visionary lives in a sleepy world between what is and what could be. The visionary does not possess all the resources to lead others. The major difference in the two is leadership ability.

Leadership is the one ingredient missing in most organizations today. Many organizations have replaced leadership with a caretaker mentality— "Let's not rock the boat and we will be fine." This will not work in today's times.

From Imagination to Reality

Developing a vision is like painting a portrait. A finely written vision statement is worthless unless the leader is living, breathing, and acting it out every day. It doesn't have to be written down, but it needs to be visible in the minds and hearts of everyone in the organization. The leader must communicate it in a way that it is understood by everyone in the organization. A good vision statement has the following ingredients:

NEED TO HAVE ONE.

Innovative organizations, like people, have a personality. Organization's without a vision are like rudderless ships being carried away with whatever storm happens to blow by. A vision aligns people's dreams with the goals of the business.

NEED TO BE CHALLENGING.

As a child I remember President Kennedy's rousing speech about going to the moon. That speech set hearts, minds, and muscles in motion. That one challenge did more than a warehouse full of strategic plans and a brigade of management consultants. It was clear to all of us where we were heading. It wasn't to the bottom of the ocean, it wasn't to the North Pole. It was to the moon!

Charles Garfield, the author of *Peak Performance*, told a story about what happened at Arlington National Cemetery the day Apollo 11 landed on the moon. Someone placed a dozen roses on President Kennedy's grave with a note. The note said, "Mr. President, the Eagle has landed."

NEED TO BE INSPIRING.

Visions of the future are the most powerful motivators in the world. People are tired of the mundane, tired of being ripped off by charlatans and self-serving individuals. People are ready for sincere, authentic leadership. An inspiring vision for the future mobilizes people into action.

NEED TO BE SHARED.

Everyone in the organization must understand what the vision is, and it has to be communicated in hundreds of ways. Roger Smith, the previous CEO of General Motors, realized the importance GM's vision statement too late. He said,

> If I had the opportunity to do everything over again, I would make exactly the same decision...But I sure wish I'd done a better job of communicating with GM people. I'd do that differently a second time around and make sure they understood and share my vision...If people understand the why, they'll understood and share my vision...If people understand the why, they'll work at it...We were, charging up the hill right on schedule, and I looked behind me and saw that many people were still at the bottom.

NEED TO UNIFY.

Nelson Mandella's vision for a free South Africa helped to destroy apartheid. His vision helped unify Africans to one cause. People want to know why they should take this trip with you, what is in it for them. Some unifying factors people look for are pride, trust, reward, opportunity, and recognition, just to name a few.

NEED TO POINT TO THE WAY.

The vision must point to the place you want to go—to the moon, to be the best, or another appropriate challenge. It provides a reference point and provides a compelling reason to change. Avoid general statements like "good," or "meet customer needs."

Making the Vision a Reality

Here are a few thoughts and questions to explore during the vision-making process:

1. **Decide what business you are in or what business you should be in.**

2. **Define the values and guiding principles taking you toward your vision.**

3. **Who will your customers and populations be in the future?**

4. **Highlight the skills you will need to reach the vision.**

5. **What will your products and services be x years from now?**

6. **Identify the major goals leading you toward the vision.**

7. **Break down each goal into key objectives.**

8. **Identify barriers and obstacles preventing accomplishment.**

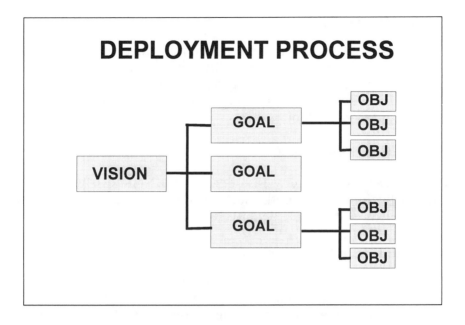

SAMPLE VISION STATEMENTS

Ft. Stewart Army Dental Activity

* To provide our customers the best dental service possible.

* To insure combat readiness for our soldiers.

* To view change as an opportunity to improve quality.

* To place customer satisfaction first.

* To empower staff members to do what is right for the customer.

St. Clair Hospital

Our Vision is to be the premier provider of health care services by exceeding the expectations of our patients, employees, physicians, volunteers, and communities.

Saturn Mission Statement

Market vehicles developed and manufactured in the United States that are world leaders in quality, cost and customer satisfaction through the integration of people, technology and business systems and to transfer knowledge, technology and experience throughout General Motors.

Fort Detrick, Maryland

Fort Detrick, a quality installation and leading community guided by innovative, enthusiastic people serving present and future needs of its people, tenants and the nation.

AT&T Universal Card Services

To be our customers' best services relationship. Consistent delivery of world-class customer service and value, achieved through long-term investment in our customers, people, and technologies.

U.S. Army Medical Command

A worldwide health delivery command providing customer-oriented quality, accessible, efficient health care while ensuring a battle-focused, trained and ready medical force to support the Department of Defense.

West Paces Medical Center, Atlanta

Be the best value health care system in Atlanta by 1996, and to be recognized as such.

Managing Along the Information Superhighway

The Scud missiles flamed toward their targets behind friendly lines in Saudi Arabia and Israel. We were in the Persian Gulf War, and Iraq unleashed another salvo of airborne lethality. Air raid sirens sent both American soldiers and journalists into their bunkers beneath the surface. At any second the missile would explode on the military base. Except for a few foolhardy reporters and a couple of remote video cameras, no one was standing in the open.

Deep underground in a protected bunker, an American soldier talked to his wife back at Ft. Benning, Georgia, via cellular phone. His wife was glued to the television watching live coverage on CNN of the same missile attack. Blow by blow, moment by moment, she relayed the information back to her husband via the cell phone. Like a military command post, she told him when the attack was over and when it was clear to return outside.

This spouse, like millions of others, has learned how to innovatively manage information. A few years ago these same electronic tools were only available to a small number of people. Today, half the modern world has access to them.

However, not everyone is as successful as the woman at Fort Benning. Compaq's customer help center gets over 8,000 calls each day. In 1993, the WordPerfect Corporation received almost four million calls to their customer support offices. Many of the people who handle these calls are like Jay Albinger, a technician at Dell Computer, who answers questions from frustrated customers like the one below.

The customer said she couldn't turn the computer on. He asked her what happened when she turned the power button on.

"I've pushed and pushed on this foot pedal and nothing happens," she said. "Foot pedal?" Jay replied. "Yes," the woman said, "this little white foot pedal with the on switch." The foot pedal she was stepping on was the mouse.

Workers face the additional demands of keeping up with the information explosion. Along with longer working hours and downsized departments, workers are trying to stay up with latest software version and the latest electronic devices. According to the American Society for Training and Development, a typical person on the job spends 1 1/2 to 2 hours a day reading charts, reports, computer screens, and other material. These demands are even greater when factoring in information sources available on the Internet.

The information available on the Internet is staggering. Employees can now turn their PCs into a library, a complete resource center. No longer do they have to run to departments and offices trying to get data and information. Not everyone is excited about the possibilities. Tom Peters shares his feelings on the situation, saying, "I'm concerned that this global cacophony will in fact be garbage at the speed of light."

Tools for a New Working World

Information remains as one of the three key elements in the innovation triad. There are as many sources of information as there are ways to manage it. By learning how to manage information effectively, business leaders will improve productivity, reduce costs, and increase efficiency. The following tools for a new working world provide insight on how to stay ahead.

TOOL 1—LEARN TO WEB.

"Webbing" means the ability to pull together groups of people and resources to get the job done. The ladder of success and longevity is disappearing in many organizations. What is becoming more important is the ability to network and get the job done. Teams form and disband to move on to the next project. Rank, pay grade, and position are becoming irrelevant in the innovative organization. As a "webber," interpersonal skills are as important as technical skills. Interpersonal skills are valuable assets that people need to bring to any organization.

TOOL 2—USE THE TECHNOLOGY.

In many cases, staying competitive and productive may depend on staying up with the latest technology. In 1990, 18 percent of the functions at Ford were controlled by computer. In 1994, it had increased to 82 percent. As individuals or as an organization, we need to know what is available to make us better and more productive. Whether it is the latest software, newest version of robotics, or better items for improved communication, we need to stand ready to apply it to our work environment.

TOOL 3—BUILD RELATIONSHIPS.

All businesses today must bridge gaps and help to provide for the interpersonal needs within the workforce. The information explosion is causing people to spend more time with a computer terminal. Stress and job pressures are taking a big toll and having negative consequences. The increase in technology requires a corresponding increase of soft-sided management. Workers are social people and still need a forum of social expression.

TOOL 4—PAINT A BIG PICTURE.

It is important to convey a challenging vision that lets everyone know how their job relates to the big picture. A vision lets the individuals within the organization know what the organization stands for, where it is heading, and how it will reach its destination. Communicate all plans, goals, and objectives to everyone within the organization.

TOOLS FOR A NEW WORKING WORLD

- **Learn to Web**
- **Use the Technology**
- **Build Relationships**
- **Paint a Big Picture**
- **Seek the Skills**

TOOL 5—SEEK THE SKILLS.

The innovative leader seeks trainers, consultants, or whatever resources are needed to keep the workforce finely tuned and capable of performing at maximum efficiency. To do this requires continuous training and education. The nation's most valuable resource is people's ideas, skills, and creative potential. Our greatest advantage comes from capitalizing on these resources.

How to Improve Communication

Information and communication are two sides of the same coin. Although the sides are connected, each remains uniquely separate. Information is the lifeblood of any enterprise. On one side of the coin there is information. Information relates to the goals, needs, plans, details, and the vision of the organization. On the other side, there is communication. Communication is the process of spreading information throughout the organization.

Management's goal is to maximize communication by providing the right types of information. Information has certain performance expectations. It has to be provided at the right time, to the right people, in the right forum. Most organizations do not spend enough time communicating. Meetings weakly attempt to provide information; however, meetings waste more time than anything else. The time people spend in meetings could have been spent working on important objectives.

In the rapidly changing environment, the right types of information and the method used to communicate information are important to the vitality of business life. Information is communicated in two directions—upward and downward. Downward communication is the process of sending information from the top to the bottom. Downward communication appears as policies, memos, regulations, directives, and such.

Upward communication is the process of gathering information from the bottom and taking it to the top. Upward communication involves more skill and a greater amount of listening. Upward communication means spending time on the front line and focusing on the issues, concerns, and problems workers are experiencing. Both forms of communication are important. One important point to remember—you can never over communicate.

Unfortunately, most traditional organizations spend far more time sending and less time listening. The innovative organization concentrates more on upward communication than downward communication. We can improve the flow of information while enhancing downward communication in many ways.

The way people process information is based on many factors. The organization of the twenty-first century is a diverse melting pot of people. These factors are determined by gender, culture, learning styles, and temperaments. Traditional ways of communication are not going to be as effective.

In fact, many enterprises have created new management positions for the sole purpose of improving communication and information. Some of these positions have names like "Director of Communication" or "Information Director." Federal Express has an employee communications department staffed with 60 people. The company provides 300 publications and 400 videos each year for their 91,000 employees. Here are a few traditional and untraditional ways to improve communication.

Downward Communication

Storytelling

In a high-tech age such as we live in, providing information using a personal approach is an effective way to improve communication. The art of storytelling existed before books, computers, and e-mail. Telling stories and using personal illustrations is a universal way to communicate ideas and information. This is particularly true when people are already in information overload. A story can help focus the abstract into a clearer picture. Storytelling crosses all boundaries, regardless of the culture, background, or position of listeners within the business. Communicating using illustrations and stories takes more time, but is a more effective way to provide important information.

Electronic Communication

In addition to storytelling, leaders must also rely on electronic communication. Electronic communication is an instantaneous way to provide information. The costs of televideo conferencing are dropping, making this method of communication more attractive to more people. Whether it is Local Area Networks, e-mail, interactive multimedia, fax machines, cellular phones, electronic forums, or others—all provide access to almost everyone in the global society.

On-line services have multiplied and offer a wide range of information. The biggest three are America Online (AOL), CompuServe, and Prodigy, with Delphi and GEnie close behind. Microsoft Mail is also entering the market. These services are more "user-friendly" than many BBSs. They have attractive interfaces with colors, and "bells and whistles," and they are easy to use through simple pull-down menus. You click on a choice with your mouse and get your wish fulfilled more or less immediately. At the end of this chapter are the major providers of on-line services along with their phone numbers.

Newsletters

Many organizational newsletters fell victim to corporate downsizings. Newsletters can turn a cold, impersonal workplace to a warmer, friendlier workplace. They remain a valuable tool for improving morale and motivation and for communicating important information in a non-threatening manner. People like to read newsletters, particularly if they include information about the people who work in the organization. They provide an excellent platform to communicate awards and recognition, births, marriages, etc. A newsletter can either be printed on paper or sent electronically to everyone in the organization.

Audio Tape

The National Speakers Association communicates to its four thousand plus members by using a monthly audio tape. NSA recognizes that many people spend a lot of time in automobiles that could be used productively. The audio tape provides all kinds of information, including interviews with other speakers, health and fitness techniques, information on upcoming events, and news important to the speaking professional.

Upward Communication

Probably the least used but most important form of communication is upward communication. A business organization is like a human being. A human is a collection of different parts that are related but function separately. In the business organization, there are separate departments, offices, and other strata. Upward communication helps to reduce the barriers between the top and the bottom, the led and the leaders. Listening is a valuable part of upward communication.

Motorola sponsors a worldwide, problem-solving team competition once a year. The goal is to encourage each site to come up with their own communication programs. This competition helps Motorola employees understand the company's strategy, gives employees an opportunity to provide feedback, and shows them how their job fits in the bigger picture. Here are a few other forms of upward communication to consider.

One-to-One Contact

Nothing can replace the interpersonal dynamic of one-to-one contact between the leader and the worker. Nothing is as powerful a tool for providing a human element within management. In this fast-paced, nonstop world, interpersonal contact is becoming more difficult, particularly in the larger businesses and organizations. All leaders should make a priority to spend time in the field, out of the office, just talking and listening to people. No agenda is needed; interaction doesn't even have to be about work. Just go talk about anything—family, pets, whatever matters to workers most.

Included in one-to-one contact is what is called, "Brown-Bag Lunches" or "Lunch with the Boss." I used to make it a habit to take soldiers out to lunch with me at the Officers Club. The Officers Clubs were open to all ranks during lunch. This was an effective tool to knock down perceptual barriers and close the gaps between rank and position, role and responsibility. This provided me a good way to get to know my soldiers on a more personal level. During these lunches, we discovered that we were all basically the same.

Town Hall Meetings

Town Hall meetings, made popular by recent political figures, is another way of providing upward access. Town Hall meetings are open to anyone who wants to attend. Businesses could use this forum to put out important information affecting everyone within the organization. Don't forget to include family members, partners, and other employee support groups in the process.

Focus Groups and Sensing Sessions

A good way to find out how people feel about a particular issue is by using focus groups or sensing sessions. If you are looking for specific answers to specific issues, this forum may be what you are looking for. When dealing with internal issues, workers are more willing to speak to an "outsider" than someone from within the organization. This is not always the case, but it is true more in the traditionally structured organization. Make sure you don't use just any "outsider." Use a trained consultant or facilitator.

Computerized Assessment Surveys

Becoming more popular is the computerized form of customer surveys, sometimes called "attitude surveys." These tools eliminate the old paper and pencil approach. Now, with ease and almost in minutes, a leader can know what people think about a multitude of areas. Surveys can be given to teams so they can evaluate the strengths and weakness of the team leader. Customized surveys can find out the attitudes of the entire organization. Another key advantage provided by many of these surveys is that they can automatically do the mathematical computations. This is important when the goal is trying to reach ISO 9000 or Malcolm Baldrige criteria.

Employee Hot Lines

Providing employees a phone line to call for information also improves bottom-up communication. Anyone can call to "vent" problems, ask questions, or get information. The service can be expanded to 24 hours a day by adding voice-mail or an answering machine. Make sure, however, that you get back to the employee in a timely manner; otherwise you could do more harm than good and damage credibility.

COMMUNICATION CHECKLIST

→ Speak regularly about the vision, mission, and goals of your department and organization.

→ Regularly hold "town meetings" to keep people informed of changes and new information.

→ Your plans should include everyone in the organization...from the lowest to the highest ranking individuals.

→ Insure that all telecommuters, distant-based, part-time workers, and volunteers are included in communication efforts.

→ Initiate procedures to insure that supervisors distribute information down to their staffs.

→ Conduct employee surveys to sample attitudes and opinions.

→ Identify what information is critical to the success and morale of the staff.

→ Create a formal plan to spread information throughout the organization.

→ Assign someone in the organization the sole responsibility of managing information. Consider creating a communications or information position.

→ **Spend a major portion of time just walking around and talking to people.**

→ **Don't hide bad news. Be up front. Rumors thrive when workers aren't kept informed.**

The Right Way to Manage Meetings

"One either meets or one works. One cannot do both at the same time." This is how Dr. Peter Drucker expresses the attitude of executives and managers toward meetings.

According to a *Wall Street Journal* survey, meetings account for the greatest amount of unproductive time—topping telephone calls, paperwork, travel, and office gossip. With a little preparation, meetings can be transformed into productive assemblies helping the business move toward, instead of away from, its goals.

The average manager spends ten hours a week in meetings. If we multiply ten hours times, say, 48 weeks, that gives us 480 hours a year spent in meetings. One *Fortune* 500 firm translated this into a $71 million loss per year in salary alone. Having said that, meetings are still the most-used communication tool in today's companies. Imagine how much time and money can be saved if only these gatherings were run a little more effectively.

Before the Meeting

The key ingredient for a good meeting is preparation. Ask yourself the following questions. Is this meeting really necessary? Can the information be put over the Local Area Network? If there is still a need for a meeting, the following points provide a blueprint for an effective conference:

1. Fix an objective or goal for the meeting.

2. Send out a one-page agenda stating the purpose, the issues to be discussed, and the time limits for each topic.

3. Determine who will participate and how each attendee needs to prepare.

4. In addition, declare a starting time AND ending time.

These simple hints go a long way towards making meetings shorter and much more effective.

During the Meeting

Whether the meeting is called to exchange information, coordinate action, motivate a team, or solve problems, it needs a leader. Lack of preparation on the part of the chairperson is inexcusable. His or her main objective is to keep things on track. Here are some easy, common-sense steps to keep in mind:

1. Start on time and do not wait for late arrivals. I once knew a boss who locked the door to the meeting room, keeping late comers standing in the hallway.

2. Allow interruptions only for genuine emergencies.

3. Discuss one issue at a time.

4. At the end of each discussion point, summarize and fix a list of "next steps": who, how, when, and where.

5. Release those participants who are no longer needed. The smaller the group, the better.

6. Above all, adhere strictly to the time constraints. If a topic needs more than the allotted time, take a vote to either re-schedule it for the next meeting or to eliminate another agenda point in its favor.

7. Control of the agenda and discussion should be firm and polite.

8. End the meeting on time.

After the Meeting

Just as important as the invitation to a conference is the follow-up. Prepare a brief summary of what was said and send it out as soon as possible. The summary should be concise and stipulate exactly what is to be done, who will do it, how it will be accomplished, and when it will be accomplished.

Meeting Facilitators

A survey revealed only 33 percent of business leaders had any training in how to effectively run meetings. In many cases, using a formally trained facilitator will improve productivity, save time, and in the end, save money.

A facilitator is particularly important in task forces, focus groups, and process action teams. A trained facilitator keeps the group on-track, helping them with decision and problem-solving techniques. Another key advantage is their impartiality. This impartiality helps to avoid the influences of rank and position that may intimidate other meeting participants. The facilitator works with the chairperson helping design the agenda, the flow of information, and the actual process of running a meeting.

The need for meetings will always exist. However, meetings may not be the most efficient way to communicate information. This is especially true in an economy that thrives on information and changes at unprecedented rates. People today are working overtime just to stay up. By managing meetings and information more efficiently, you will positively impact the bottom line.

Contact Information	
CompuServe	800/848-8199, 614/457-0802
America Online	800/827-6364, 703/448-8700
GEnie	800/638-9636, 301/251-6415
Dow Jones News/Retrieval	800/522-3567, 609-452-1511
Delphi Internet Services	800/695-4005, 617/491-3342
Prodigy	800/776-2339

CHAPTER 8

BUILDING A FOUNDATION FOR THE FUTURE

"My interest is in the future...because I'm going to spend the rest of my life there."

—Charles Kettering

America's public school system gets blamed for many deficiencies, some deserved, some not. Our school systems have come a long way, but we are still falling short—we are not changing fast enough.

President Clinton attended an economic conference at Emory University in Atlanta. Along with the President Clinton, many other economic and political heads of state expressed their feelings about the education system in America. Donald Ratajczak, Director of Economic Forecasting at Georgia State University, expressed his opinion. According to the *Atlanta Journal-Constitution*, Rzatajczak said, "...our elementary and secondary schools are, quite frankly, are not creating the product necessary to meet the employment needs of the jobs we are currently creating."

Education leads to success. A quality education provides the primary advantage leading to personal and business success in the world today. Our children's educational experience, both at home and school, plays the primary role in building self-esteem, developing social interaction skills, and preparing children for their future roles as responsible adults.

Heroine of Education Reform

Recognizing this fact is one of America's leading authorities on education, Mary Hatwood Futrell, an African-American woman who is devoting her life to revitalizing the public education system. Mary has the answers to many of America's education problems. One answer is—education is cheaper than incarceration.

Mary recognized the importance of education at a very early age. Her father died when she was four years old, leaving her mother as her sole guardian. To meet expenses, her mother cleaned homes and churches. They were so poor her mother was unable to afford shoes for her children. With or without shoes, with or without money, Mary's mother sent her to school.

Mary tells the story of the day she was sent home from school because she was not wearing shoes. When Mary walked home that day, her mother angrily said, "It doesn't matter what you wear or what you have, that's not important. What is important is that you get a good education." From this time on, Mary's life has been a beacon of light. She struck out to provide as many people as possible the best education this country can provide.

Mary began her professional career teaching in Alexandria, Virginia. She graduated from Virginia State College and George Washington University. During her career, she was elected President of the Virginia Education Association. Beginning in 1983, she was elected to three consecutive terms as President of the National Education Association (NEA), the nation's largest professional organization. In 1990, she would go on as the elected President of the World Confederation of Organizations of the Teaching Professionals. This organization represents over 11 million teachers throughout the world in 111 countries. She received many awards, including the American Black Achievement Award. She is listed in the *Who's Who of American Women* and has received the Anne and Leon Schull Award for Democratic Action, along with the NAACP President's Award.

Education or Incarceration?

Her impact is felt on controversial topics affecting busing, school reform, school tuition credits, and job opportunities for high school graduates. Talking about educational improvements and education reform, she says, "you either pay now or pay later." Building more prisons does not solve the crime problem, just as adding more police officers fails to reduce violence. Educating children today costs about $4,700 a year. It costs approximately $27,000 a year to put a person in jail. Building more schools, providing both jobs and opportunities, reforming the judicial system, and holding parents accountable might help improve the crime and violence problem.

She feels that by investing in education today, we can cut welfare in the future. Her message is simple and powerful—education is still the key to success no matter what color you are. However, she is quick to add that hard work will not be the only thing needed to succeed in the America of the future. "The whole emphasis is going to be on critical thinking skills, being able to use information in a highly technological society, working in teams, and understanding not only the immediate community in which you live, but also the global society...You're going to have to rely on your gray cells."

Mary Futrell is a positive catalyst for education reform. In a must-read speech she delivered called, "Cooperation for Educational Excellence, The Key to Economic Revival," she accurately outlines the realities youth face today. We need innovative leaders like Mary Futrell, who can build a new foundation for the future.

The Future of Business Begins with Kindergarten

The family and the school system are the two most influential institutions affecting the business world. I once heard a political cartoonist say, "Nothing is too small to blow totally out of proportion." When it comes to our public school system, a lot has been blown out of proportion. I think the media, and the citizens of America, have been slightly off target with their comments about our schools. Don't get me wrong, I'll be the first to agree there is much room for improvement.

As the sun rises in the morning, each day teachers prepare lesson plans and give their lives to make a difference. There are far more excellent teachers than bad ones. It's time to tell those professional educators and staff how much we appreciate what they do. It is time to quit blaming and start changing. I'd like to see a new bumper sticker that says, "I'm proud to be a teacher."

However, the U.S. school system itself does deserve some criticism. It is not the individuals, but the system they must work within. Yes, other industrialized nations have students spend more time in classes and may take education more seriously. Yes, curriculums need restructuring. Yes, we need to change the education process if we are going to stay competitive. To fix the system requires a cooperative effort from all of us. For the moment, let's take off the boxing gloves, get off the soap boxes, and look at one school in particular—the school my children go to.

Robert Fulghum's book, *All I Ever Knew I Learned in Kindergarten,* provides more truth than I've ever realized. Let me share an experience I had with my two kids, my kindergartener and my fifth grader, not too long ago.

I guarantee eating lunch with a bunch of elementary kids will positively change your outlook on life. It's a great feeling to see so much enthusiasm and optimism—all those little eyes and giggles directed toward my direction. I never got this much attention at home! Sitting at the lunch table with all these kids makes me feel younger. Life doesn't seem quite so serious. Time with these kids is better than any prescription you can get from a physician.

The Foundation of the Future

Within the classrooms, the hallways, the playgrounds, and the school yards lives the future of America. Positive results come from those parents involved with their children's education. The child becomes more proud, more confident, and takes school more seriously, improving their chances for future success. There are exceptions, but nonetheless, I feel it's very important to spend time with kids at school as often as possible. So, how does kindergarten influence the foundation of the future?

There are three indisputable factors we must understand. You cannot have quality workers without a quality education system. You cannot have a quality education system without a quality home life. Each of these factors are interrelated. Yes, the chain is only as strong as its weakest link.

Everything begins at the home. Someone much wiser than I once said, "The person who rocks the cradle rules the world." I do not pretend to be a family expert, but I do have many years of experience raising three children. Of course, my wife gets most of the credit. I also have 24 years of business experience working with adults. So given my experience and the advice of several teachers, here are seven golden rules that will improve your child's education.

☺ Read to your children every day.

☺ Review their school work and show your interest.

☺ Eat lunch with them from time to time.

☺ Sit and ask them how their day went. Be specific with your questions.

☺ Volunteer to read a story or do a class project.

☺ Limit the amount and types of television programs they watch.

☺ Open the lines of communication with your child's teacher.

To many of us, these golden rules are obvious, but nonetheless, bear repeating. Spending time at schools and showing interest in school work at home does not come easy when trying to balance both homelife and career. However, time invested in this endeavor not only will you improve your children's ability to learn, but also improves their chances of success in the ever changing world of work.

The responsibility for our children's education is shared by many institutions. It's clear that parents have the most important job when it comes to influencing their children's future, but it doesn't stop there. Moreover, teachers, the school system, and businesses all across America share in this responsibility.

Let's face it, complaining is cheap and easy. To make a difference, we must remember John F. Kennedy's famous words: "Ask not what the country can do for you, but what you can do for your country." See you in the lunchroom.

Electronic Summer Camp

What are you going to do with your kids this summer? Send them to Camp Willy Walki, soccer camp, Europe? Try something different this summer. Why don't you send them to a place where they can gain something substantial. How about sending them to computer summer camp? This is a place where they can have fun and gain a sense of achievement and possibly improve their school work.

Preparing children for the future is an important part of our role in life. Sports and athletics play a major role in children's development by teaching teamwork and discipline. However, sports gets more attention than it deserves. It disproportionately fills newspaper pages, and athletics only goes so far when providing jobs for most Americans.

On the other hand, computers and computer technology open more doors. Mastery of computer skills provides children with a competitive advantage in school and in life. I'm sad to report most schools across America still get failing grades in computer literacy. By the time computers show up in classrooms, the equipment is as obsolete as two-day-old pizza. Compounding the problem, many school teachers are themselves unfamiliar with the latest software. Many teachers depend on volunteers to teach the kids. Computer literacy should not be relegated to one teacher in the computer lab. This is a sad state of affairs when you realize computer literacy is the driving force in the business world.

This is where Futurekids answers the mail. Futurekids currently operates 400 Franchises in 50 countries around the world. The company teaches 100,000 children per month in more than 1,500 locations. Futurekids has developed important partnerships with major players in the computer industry—Microsoft, Apple, Disney, CompuServe, Egghead Software, and others—helping the company stay on the leading edge.

Programs offered at Futurekids computer learning centers provide children a solid foundation of learning skills by familiarizing them with the power of computers. In the learning centers, classes are weekly and are intentionally kept small to emphasize individualized instruction. Their goal is not simply to teach students, "...but to create students who are learners."

Futurekids offers interesting programs on topics of hardware, keyboarding skills, telecommunication, desktop publishing, spreadsheets, robotics, and graphics. They even offer week-long summer camps on a variety of subjects. Richard Miller, Director of Futurekids in Conyers, Georgia, says, "Unlike other summer camps, Futurekids' offerings promise kids not only lots of fun, but also a summer of learning and discovery that will benefit them for the rest of their lives." Kids can learn how to go on-line and find a pen pal in Hawaii. They can learn to design a new house, a space ship, or a bestselling book. The titles of these summer camps are as innovative as their content. "Robotics," "Junior Entrepreneur," "Storybook Maker," "Space Adventure," "Dinomania," and "Rapid Fire Keyboarding," sound like just what the doctor ordered.

Believe me, the skills these kids learn today will pay big dividends tomorrow. Just think, now your kids can do research for that upcoming report at home on your home computer. You won't have to take them to the library Sunday afternoon when you want to watch the game. Start investing now in your children's computer education—don't let your kids become a roadkill on the information superhighway.

Employee Benefit Plans for Working Parents

The successful manager of the 1990s and beyond is the one who can attract and keep the best qualified employees. Salaries, perks, and job security have been a motivating force in the past, but things are different today. Family-oriented benefits are high on the totem pole for today's newbreed workforce. Child care is a major concern for working parents. The resourceful manager must realize the importance of employee benefit plans in keeping and attracting the best qualified employees.

Dramatic influences have changed the attitudes within America's workforce. Changing social values and lifestyles are forcing their way into business. More than ever, more women, working mothers, dual career couples, and single parents are entering the workforce.

With the increase of working parents, there is an increased need for more childcare services. In 1991, close to 42 percent of the working mothers had children age 18 or younger, while 60 percent of the working mothers have children under the age of six. Parents deposit their children at child care facilities, day care centers, and private homes. Most arrangements result in a quilt work of frustrating, stressful, and often, inconvenient arrangements.

Issues Affecting Working Women

As more and more women enter the workforce, many of the best qualified women are exiting the back door. There are many reasons why. Some leading causes include organizational rigidity, unequitable pay differences with male counterparts, and their own unrealistic expectations. Other than pay differences, Allen Cox, a Chicago-based executive recruiter, says the demands of raising a family is the most significant reason why women are leaving the workforce.

Pay issues comprise a major issue for many women. A salary comparison made at PIT between MBA women and MBA men show major differences. Women earned an average of $9,000 less than men from the same graduating class.

On the other hand, there is some good news on the horizon. The gap between men and women's pay may be narrowing. Other data shows 48 percent of employed married women earn as much as their husbands. Recent research by Louis Harris & Associates for the Families and Work Institute showed 55 percent of 1,502 working women said their salaries made up half or more of the family income.

Family Work Issues

Successful businesses realize family life directly affects the innovative ability of all organizations. Businesses who ignore the impact of family life on work will suffer. Companies are realizing that to attract and keep the best employees, they must respond to their needs as both employees and parents.

Family life, especially child care responsibilities, can result in high absenteeism, high turnover, lack of dedication, and decreased productivity. A manager who can provide family benefits will not only improve his relations with his employees, but simultaneously improve their dedication and productivity.

In August 1993, the Family Leave Act was ratified, which requires companies to allow employees to take up to 12 weeks of unpaid leave for birth, adoption, or a seriously ill family member. All public agencies and private firms with fifty or more employees who work within a 75-mile radius must comply with this law.

A 1992 study by Philadelphia benefits consultants, Hay/Huggins, found that 36 percent of large U.S. companies now offer flexible-hours policies, 14 percent have telecommuting programs, and almost half allow paternity leave. The U.S. Conference Board estimates that several hundred U.S. firms now have work/family managers, most of whom have been hired within the last two years, to develop and administer benefits for parents.

At one time, American Express had an attrition rate of 20 percent. Their workforce was 73 percent female. Their research showed it cost them approximately $27,000 to replace each worker. The cost included recruitment, orientation, and down time associated with continuity. Today, using more flexible practices, the company reduced attrition to 9 percent.

Unions, feeling the pressure of losing membership, are also adjusting. To attract working women, unions are now improving benefits by providing adjusted career ladders for women, child care, and parental leave policies. The American Federation of State, County and Municipal Employees has provided parental leave policies in 85 union contracts covering 755,000 workers.

Child Care Worries

Child care worries cause parents to think more about their children than their work. A survey of 8,000 employees from 22 different companies showed that 59 percent of female workers with kids under age 12 had problems finding child care. Women with kids under 12 missed an average of 12 days of work each year. Many parents make child care changes 2–3 times a year. Working men who either had a partner or another adult at home only missed eight days a year.

Another factor that negatively affects work time has become known as the "three o'clock syndrome." This refers to a particular time of the day when accidents increase and productivity decreases because employees worry about their kids when they get out of school. A survey, conducted by John P. Fernandez, AT&T personnel services manager, found that 77 percent of women and 78 percent of men handle family issues on the phone at the job. To help counter this situation, KCTV-Channel 5 in Kansas City, Missouri, established PhoneFriend in 1984. PhoneFriend is a community-sponsored reassurance program for "latchkey" children. Volunteers answer telephone lines 3 P.M.–6 P.M. during the school year and 9 A.M.–6 P.M. during the summer. Children call these "warmlines" for care, reassurance, and other non-emergency matters. PhoneFriend averaged 60 calls a day during the school year, and 70 calls a day during the summer. All the calls were from kids. Kansas City claimed this program has been "enormously successful."

Child Care Benefits

The combined impact of family life on the job can be either tremendously positive or devastating to the workplace. There have been many programs placed into effect that have countered the work/family conflicts and gained significant positive results. Many of the services balance the need of the worker with that of cost to the employer.

Child care benefits are viewed differently by parents than other forms of compensation. Because working parents are concerned about their children, family benefits will experience the greater growth in the next decade. They want more than a babysitting service, they want quality care.

The most popular benefit is direct child care services. Despite various attitudes toward it, studies have shown that employer-assisted child care services significantly reduce turnover and absenteeism. In a study done by the Sioux Valley Hospital in Sioux Falls, South Dakota, turnover was reduced by 7.8 percent annually. This represented an annual savings of $159,000.

On-Site Services. Company-run or on-site child care services are the most popular with employees, but can cause significant concerns for managers. Hospitals have been the most successful at implementing such programs, primarily because it was the best way to adapt to various shift work and to counter the nursing shortage. In The Mercy Richards Hospital of Bakersfield, California, such as program reduced turnover by 56 percent, reduced tardiness by 64 percent, and improved productivity by 42 percent. Morale improved tremendously. Reduction in turnover alone saved $84,000 in costs.

Despite the excellent results with on-site child care, there are some significant drawbacks. Most businesses are concerned with the cost of building an on-site center, in addition to the liability and insurance costs.

Off-Site Services. Off-site child care facilities are the more common benefit provided to workers by business. Many centers are subsidized by employers. Employers also provide referral services, child care financial assistance, and child care consortiums.

A successful off-site center is sponsored by the American Savings and Loan Association of Stockton, California. It is called, Little Mavericks School of Learning. This is a "top-of-the-line" program that was expensive to start but has almost paid for itself. In fact, Little Maverick's subsidization costs less than American Savings' corporate coffee service. The school is five blocks from the main headquarters. This well organized program provides many options for employees. Options include holiday care, Boy Scout and Girl Scout activities, sick child care, and other popular programs.

Information and referral services. Smaller businesses who cannot afford on-site or subsidized off-site care can provide information and referral services. One employee's job can be totally dedicated to obtaining and coordinating child care services for employees of the company. Another option is to contract with a local child care development organization providing this type of service. This service can be further complemented by adding family seminars and conferences.

Financial assistance. Providing extra money is an even simpler program that avoids the liability. Employees are free to choose any type of service that is either more convenient or best suited to their needs. The employer will reimburse the employee at either cost or partial cost.

Consortium. Two or more companies can group together and form a consortium. This is less expensive than either an on-site or near-site center. This is more popular in industrial or office parks. This program provides a variety of services from financial assistance to child care referrals.

Flextime. Flexible work schedules can lessen the need for outside dependency on child care arrangements. Commonly called Flextime or Flexitime, it comes in several variations. The most common arrangement allows employees to come and go 1–2 hours before or after a set core time period. The core time, for example, is 10 A.M.–3 P.M. Other variations allow employees to work longer hours one day and shorter hours the next.

Some companies even allow employees to take work home with them. Other companies provide office support including computers. More businesses are going to four 10-hour work days giving employees a 3-day weekend. Shacklee Corporation allows some of its employees to negotiate a shorter work week with their supervisors allowing them to spend more time at home. The employees are only paid for what they work, but do not lose seniority or any other benefits.

Job sharing is becoming more popular. Two or more workers can share the same job. Job sharing works for either blue and white collar jobs. Job sharing was first initiated at Steelcase Inc. in Grand Rapids, Michigan. They discovered it brought many benefits to the company. Job sharing lowered absenteeism and turnover. It also positively helped reach Affirmative Action Goals allowing more minorities to work. Cal Jetter, Steelcase's director of Employee Information and Services, said, "It allows us to retain valued employees who want to go to part-time and would otherwise leave."

Job sharing has problems. It is more expensive in that there is more administrative overhead with the continuation and pro-rating of benefits. Despite the additional costs, the positive results contribute to a more loyal and motivated workforce.

Telecommuting. The traditional 9-to-5 work schedule is not for everyone. When faced with long commute times and the cost of office space, frequently organizations are turning to telecommuting. Many businesses are providing this option as a reward or incentive to their best workers.

In July of 1995, CNN conducted an informal survey of the St. Paul Company that offers flexible maternity leave from 12 weeks to 6 months. They provide in-home computer terminals so their employees can stay in contact with their offices. The result is that most women take much less than six months leave and become the most loyal employees the company can ask for.

Telecommuting is ideal for some but not for others. Many workers still need the social aspects of going to work. Other telecommuters feel disadvantaged when it comes to promotions because of the "out of sight/out of mind" syndrome. Nonetheless, telecommuting is rapidly becoming the work lifestyle of the twenty-first century.

With increasing numbers of working women and more single-parent families, family benefits are a crucial issue of importance. Balancing the needs of working parents is mutually beneficial to companies and employees.

CHAPTER 9

CREATING THE HIGH PERFORMANCE ORGANIZATION

"There is less to fear from outside competition than from inside inefficiency, discourtesy and bad service."

—Anonymous

How long does it take your business to process an order? How many of your customers are dissatisfied with your service? Are your employees properly trained to do their jobs? Are you continuously improving everything your business does? If you can't answer these questions, you need to read this chapter.

Putting Quality to Work

L.L. Bean correctly ships 99.9 percent of all its orders, even during Christmas. Iomega reduced cycle time on it's computer disk drive manufacturing process from 28 days to 1.5 days. In six years De Mar Plumbing and Air Conditioning went from $210,000 to $3.5 million in sales. In 1992 the Saturn automobile rated third in customer satisfaction according to J.D. Powers and Associates. What do all these companies have in common? They successfully put quality management principles to work improving their businesses.

Few management philosophies have made such a tremendous impact on business than that of Total Quality Management (TQM), or its counterpart called, Continuous Quality Improvement (CQI). Advocates have hailed TQM as the way to improve productivity, regain business lost to competition, and improve worker participation. For many organizations, TQM has meant survival.

Along with its evangelical supporters, TQM has its critics. In fact, the critics have probably sounded the loudest trumpets. Many have claimed TQM is a passing fad, an expensive program that fails to generate results. I hope to clarify what these three initials represent in the following discussion.

What is TQM?

TQM has one goal—to tap the potential, abilities, skills, and knowledge laying dormant in the workforce. Many people have a narrow opinion of TQM. In my mind, TQM is the combination and consolidation of the world's best management tools and techniques under one management umbrella. It is a way of integrating everything a business or organization should do to stay successful. It applies to all types of organizations, to all types of industries. TQM is not a fad or program. Nor is it what many people simplistically call, "common sense management."

It is a management system for achieving exceptional customer satisfaction by involving everyone in the business. One of its major underpinnings is the focus placed on how work is performed, called process management. By focusing on the work process, businesses insure they do the right things right, and reduce waste, rework, and expensive, unproductive work procedures. By incorporating basic statistics and key performance indicators, the business continuously improves everything the customer considers important. Total Quality Management has the following key characteristics.

Key Characteristics

→ **Customer-Driven Focus.** TQM places the customer in the center of the universe. The business strives to meet and exceed the customer's needs and expectations.

There are both internal customers (employees) and external customers.

→ **Continual Improvement.** Demands continual improvement in all areas. William Perry, past Executive Director, Quality Assurance Institute, said, "If quality is not improving, it's deteriorating." TQM is a long-term, never ending process.

→ **Prevention Orientation.** TQM substitutes inspection with prevention and elimination of problems. By eliminating the root causes of problems, prevention lowers costs by reducing rework, dissatisfied customers, recalls, and defective products.

→ **Team Approach.** TQM relies on teams to reengineer, solve, and prevent work problems. Everyone, including suppliers, management, workers, and customers become equal partners in the improvement process.

→ **Employee Empowerment.** Quality management requires special training and a unified effort from everyone in the business. Productivity comes through harnessing the ideas and energy of all people at all levels. Management provides the resources, training, and support to get the job done.

→ **Process Management.** A process is a series of related steps leading to a particular outcome. It follows a structured, problem-solving approach instead of the typical "knee-jerk" type of decision making. It uses facts and data to bring important functions under control. The diagram that follows shows the process tasks and the interrelationship between the supplier and the customer.

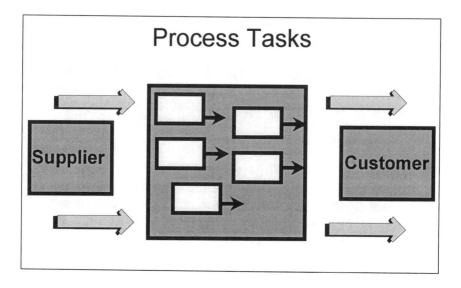

Background

One of the world's most widely known quality experts was the late Dr. Edwards Deming. Working as a statistician for the U.S. government, he traveled to Japan at the end of WW II. His teachings had a tremendous effect on the Japanese economy, which was destroyed by the war. In thirty years or less, Japan went from a country making trinkets from discarded beer cans to an industrial giant manufacturing luxury automobiles, VCRs, and flat screen television sets.

Dr. Deming traveled back and forth to Japan teaching them statistical process control and management principles based on what would later become his 14 points of management. Deming's 14 points constitute the core of his recommendations to management for achieving quality excellence.

1. Create constancy of purpose for the improvement of product and service.

2. Adopt the new philosophy.

3. Cease dependence on mass inspection.

4. End the practice of awarding business on price tag alone.

5. Improve constantly and forever the system of production and service.

6. Institute training and retraining.

7. Institute leadership.

8. Drive out fear.

9. Break down barriers between staff areas.

10. Eliminate slogans, exhortations, and targets for the work force.

11. Eliminate numerical quotas.

12. Remove barriers to pride of workmanship.

13. Institute a vigorous program of education and retraining.

14. Take action to accomplish the transformation.

The Journey Along the Quality Highway

While Japan rebuilt its economy, America was sleeping. We finally woke up in the 80s, only to realize we were almost three decades behind. America has been running in a heated race to catch up since then.

Most organizations do not completely understand TQM, while others have made revolutionary improvements. Companies such as Saturn Corporation, Motorola, Ford Motor Company, FedEx, Johnson & Johnson, and Ritz-Carlton Hotels have used TQM to great advantage. Since the 80s, businesses such as these have come a long way down the quality highway.

In recent years, TQM made its sweep into the service sector and into many classrooms across America. Healthcare organizations, such as West Paces Ferry Hospital in Atlanta, have moved to a quality-centered, customer-focused work environment. Surprisingly, even the military has signed-up, seeing the benefits. The result has truly been a "quality revolution," but it still hasn't gone far enough.

The Missing Ingredient

My favorite story is the fabled race between the hare and the turtle. The hare quickly learned that success doesn't necessarily go to the swiftest, just the smartest. Businesses in America must learn the same lesson.

During the past twenty years, thousands upon thousands of business books and hundreds of new business philosophies have taken shelf space in libraries. Quality management, work teams, participative management, outdoor wilderness trips, business process reengineering, and countless other philosophies and programs

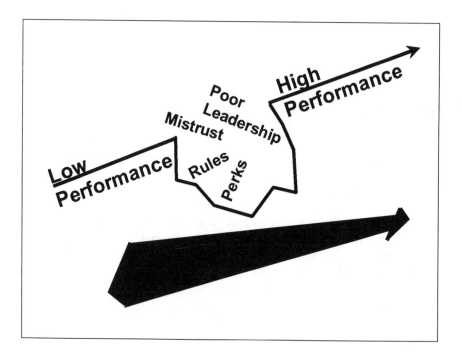

beckon us. Some of these efforts have potential. Many had limited success, but the majority have done more harm than good.

The road along the quality journey is littered with mistakes and shipwrecks of the well meaning but misguided. A careful diagnosis reveals most failures were not due to a faulty philosophy, but tied to a faulty strategy. There were one or more key elements missing. These missing elements created a gap between low performance and high performance. Something was missing. Traditional organizations cannot be led by teams, committees, and boards. The ingredient linking all the elements is strong, committed, and effective leadership. Someone must steer the ship. Action is more important than philosophy.

One person I worked with had a favorite saying. He said, "Autocratic clarity is better than participative fuzziness." Don't get me wrong—teams, focus groups, and participative management serve important purposes. But without a strong and effective leader, all management philosophies are doomed to failure. We cannot let philosophies, programs, and textbook approaches replace authentic, action-oriented leadership.

Keys to Success

TQM is not a magic potion. It can't be sprinkled on people like pixie dust. There are no silver bullets...just hard work and the proper application of key principles. My experience with many different types of businesses, backed by the input of hundreds of people, shaped the following key principles. These key principles will help you avoid the traps and pitfalls of putting quality to work:

KEY 1:   TOP MANAGEMENT'S INVOLVEMENT AND COMMITMENT.

This is the most important key. Without strong commitment and active involvement from the chain of command, TQM will become just another program, a flavor of the month—here today and gone tomorrow.

KEY 2:   CAREFUL PLANNING.

A builder never lays the first brick without the architect's plans. Spending the time at first to develop a strategy, methodology, and a road map is critically important. The implementation plan, as a minimum, spells out how fast to go, what projects to tackle, who has what responsibility, how people will be trained, etc. The plan connects the vision and strategic plan with the goals and objectives of the organization. Without a plan, all the ideas, activities, and results quickly lose momentum, becoming unmanageable.

KEY 3:   CUSTOMER FOCUS.

All efforts focus on improving customer service to both internal and external customers. Internal customers are the workers within the company. External customers are the ones who actually pay for the service or product. The people in charge must identify the customer's requirements and design a system to meet their needs. If the customer can't feel, see, smell, taste, or experience what you are doing, you are wasting your efforts. Training should address the needs of the internal customer and the needs of the organization, as well as foster personal growth.

KEY 4:   REWARD THE NEW BEHAVIOR.

Make evangelical efforts rewarding the behavior you want. Change poses a major difficulty for most people until the new behavior becomes habit. Make it worthwhile for people to change. If you want teamwork, you must reward team behavior and minimize traditional reward and recognition.

KEY 5:   IMPLEMENTATION TEAM.

Getting the right people involved initially speeds up the implementation process. The implementation team should include a wide spectrum of people from the company, including upper management, workers, and possibly even some external customers. This group should work with a consultant to develop the implementation plan.

KEY 6:   MEASURE, MEASURE, MEASURE.

Continued success depends on measurable results. Change is difficult, and unless people can see the results, they are likely to return to old ways of doing things. Begin measuring improvements immediately. Can you show faster cycle time? Has morale improved? Is waste reduced? Link results to the bottom line and publicly post the results for all to see.

KEY 7:   GO FOR THE RESULTS.

Many implementation strategies involve lots of activities and very little results. Idea campaigns are excellent ways to increase energy and enthusiasm. People get to see results, making them more supportive of initiatives generally.

KEY 8:   SUCCESSFUL PILOT PROJECTS.

Picking big projects too soon or spending too much time on projects that don't matter are dangerous pitfalls to successful implementation. Gain energy and confidence before tackling bigger and more complex projects. Solve obvious problems first. Do an organizational or departmental assessment soon to identify issues and problems. The workforce will be more supportive and willing when their immediate issues and concerns alleviated.

KEY 9:   INVOLVE MIDDLE MANAGEMENT.

The organization must involve middle management immediately. Without the support and cooperation of this group, many projects will fail. The biggest power base is in the middle management ranks. Middle management controls most of the people in the organization.

KEY 10:   ROLE OF THE CONSULTANT.

There are two types of consultants—external and internal. Both are valuable partners to the implementation process. The value of external consultants is not just their technical expertise, but their neutrality and their credibility as "experts." A good external consultant is not politically sensitive. They can ask those important questions and address critical issues the internal consultant maybe uncomfortable with.

KEY 11:   AVOID BUILDING A QUALITY BUREAUCRACY.

Avoid creating separate offices and departments to do strategic planning, CQI/TQM, teams, reengineering, innovation etc. In my opinion, TQM should include all the above efforts. Consolidate all change agents, process managers, and quality and planning activities under one office.

KEY 13:   STRATEGIC FOCUS.

All activities, actions, teams, etc. need to be working on projects related to the vision or mission of the organization. Major improvements come from a project by the project improvement approach. Avoid the temptation to create too many teams doing too many unrelated activities.

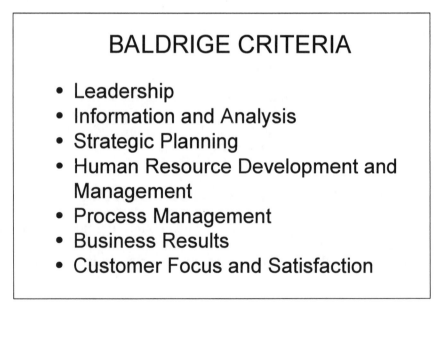

BALDRIGE CRITERIA

- Leadership
- Information and Analysis
- Strategic Planning
- Human Resource Development and Management
- Process Management
- Business Results
- Customer Focus and Satisfaction

Many organizations struggle with what the "best" organization should look like. A good organization goes beyond more than mere profits or a good reputation. Is there a structured approach, a menu of characteristics? The Malcolm Baldrige National Quality Award (NBNQA) criteria provides the framework (see Appendix B). It also provides an organized way of measuring the internal capacity of the organization as it relates to customer satisfaction. The major components helping to create a quality environment are listed in the following fishbone diagram.

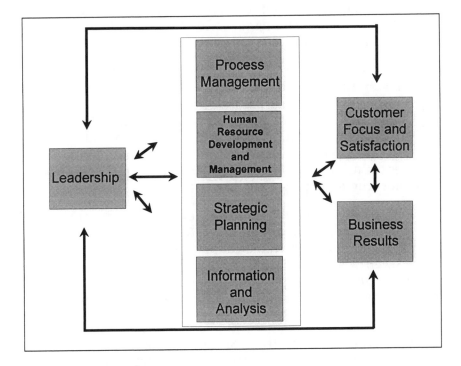

Teaming Up with Teamwork

Imagine driving to work early one day to complete a special project. As you enter the building, you hear excited voices flowing down the hall. As you walk through the office door, Mary, your Sales Manager, notices the expression on your face. She says, "Hi boss! I took care of that assignment you gave me yesterday, and it is running great. We will exceed our sales goals again this year!"

You see your office staff huddled around a table working on the proposal to improve customer service. They came in early to work on the project. Ceiling lights illuminate the charts and bar graphs showing progress made during the past year. There are no walls or offices that separate your workers from each other. The room is full of energy—a charged, innovative environment of motivated team members. They are proud of themselves and their accomplishments.

The advantages of using workplace teams and team-building cannot be overemphasized in creating the innovative work environment. In a rapidly changing world that values high-technology, speed, and flexibility, teams are providing the key ingredient for success and fostering innovation.

Teams and teamwork have improved morale, reduced costs, and dramatically improved productivity in businesses across the world. William J. O'Brian, CEO of Hanover Insurance Company, says, "The fundamental movement in business in the next 25 years will be in dispersing of power, to give meaning and fulfillment to employees in a way that avoids chaos and disorder." Teamwork is one major way to empower employees.

Teams have decreased the need for excessive layers of middle managers and supervisors. Aetna Life & Casualty increased the ratio between workers and middle management from one supervisor for seven workers to one supervisor for thirty workers, while improving customer service. At a General Mills' plant in Lodi, California, productivity escalated to 40 percent above comparable plants because of teams.

Johnsonville Foods located in Sheboygan Falls, Wisconsin, has been a flagship of productivity improvement. Almost 90 percent of the workforce belongs to some type of team. The team, not management, decides who is hired, who is fired, and who gets a pay raise. Ralph Stayer, Johnsonville's Chief Executive Officer, reports that his workers produce more sausage than he ever thought possible. His company's productivity has risen by at least 50 percent since 1986. Not only has productivity improved, but teamwork has made a tremendous impact on the morale of the company.

A twelve-person team from FedEx saved the company almost $1 million in one and one-half years by revamping a sorting process used for overnight deliveries. Another excellent example of teamwork is Allina, a health care organization located in Minnesota. One of their teams came up with an idea that saved the company $200,000 a year. They decided it was cheaper and more efficient to have hospital equipment maintained by hospital staff instead of using outside contractors.

Making Teams Work

In the early, predawn hours, a U.S. Army Special Forces team drops in by parachute into a foreign country. Hours before the invasion, they move undetected down the darkened streets, heading for a rendezvous point. Their mission is to destroy the emergency warning system surrounding the city. The American task force awaits silently in ships off the coast. Months of preparation, rehearsals, and planning lead up to this event.

The Special Forces team is one of the most highly trained and skilled teams in the world, a model for what many businesses are trying to achieve in their businesses today—a self-directed work team (SDWT). Businesses do not need to parachute into enemy territory to accomplish their mission. However, the military has provided businesses with valuable lessons and experience on the art of teamwork.

Jon Katzenbach and Douglas Smith in their book, *The Wisdom of Teams*, provide an excellent definition a team.

> *A team is a small number of people with complementary skills who are committed to a common purpose, performance goals, and approach for which they hold themselves mutually accountable.*

By paying close attention to this definition, we gain a clear understanding of the key ingredients for team success.

→ **Small Number of People.** A team usually consists of 6–12 people. Any more than this becomes difficult to manage.

→ **Complementary Skills.** Each person on the team possesses a particular skill or talent. When blended, these talents and skills improve the capability of the team. In a high performing team, team members can perform each other's skills.

→ **Committed Participants.** People do not reach maximum performance unless they are committed and trust management and each other. The dynamic human issues are critical to team success. Until team members learn to trust each other and understand each other's personalities and individual work styles, they will not become committed to the project.

→ **Common Purpose.** Most teams work on a particular project, task, or particular type of work. Committees are not teams. The most effective teams are ones that have a written charter outlining a clear goal, purpose, and mission.

→ **Common Approach.** You can't throw some people into a room and expect them to become an effective and productive team. Not having a structured way of doing work is one major reason teams fail. The most productive teams follow a standardized methodology for solving problems, designing a new service, and/or improving a process. Initially, teams require extensive training, mentoring, and coaching.

Types of Teams

Don't make the mistake of thinking all teams are the same. There are many different types of teams, permanent and temporary, simple or complex. Temporary teams, sometimes called Process Action Teams (PAT) or Quality Improvement Teams (QIT), meet to specifically work on one process or on one problem. The opposite end of the spectrum is the mother of all teams, the Self-Directed Work Team (SWDT).

The SDWT is self-contained and functions independently. This team works together permanently, such as on an assembly line or on product development. The SDWT reduces the need for an expensive and separate supervisory management chain. Team members schedule their work hours, supervise themselves, and sometimes assume responsibility for handling disciplinary matters.

There are many other types of teams, such as Quality Circles, Radical Action Teams (RAT), Key Action Teams (KAT), and Quality Improvement Teams (QIT). The BOSE Company, a manufacturer of high quality loudspeakers, have BIT teams (BOSE Improvement Teams). The job of management is to use the right team for the right job.

A special team of obstetric nurses I learned about was clearly focused on their mission. They were proud of their skills and abilities and developed their own unique T- shirt with this slogan.

TEAM W.H.O.N

Women's Health Obstetrics & Neonatal

AT YOUR

CERVIX

"Others promise but we deliver"

Worker Empowerment That Works

In an earlier life I managed six dental clinics. I had grown increasingly frustrated with our employee-of-the-month program. Once a month, the dental chiefs from the six dental clinics gathered to vote on the "best" employee. Each dentist wrote a justification about the person he thought should win. We all assembled in the main conference room to vote for one lucky person. The "winner" received a savings bond, becoming the "Employee of the Month." After several months, I noticed a trend or indication of a growing problem.

The symptoms were many. The first symptom was the attitude of Employee of the Month, the winner. Winning the award didn't seem to make a big impact on the awarded individual. The other employees also didn't seem to care who won. I examined the whole selection process.

Who were we fooling? The entire program and the method for deciding who won was unfair and biased. I discovered the only people nominated were the ones who worked the closest with their boss. Adding to the frustration, instead of the best employee getting the award, each clinic arbitrarily rotated who won each month. If clinic A won it one month, then clinic B had to win the next month. No clinic could win two months in a row. To my amazement, the award had little to do with who was the best. It only had to do with whose turn it was and who worked the closest with the boss. What about the shuttle driver, the custodians, and those other behind-the-scenes people who really needed the money? I was throwing away money and spending countless hours each month running a meaningless program. All the employees thought this program was a joke—they were right, too.

It was time to change. We formed a problem-solving team. We asked for volunteers—one from each clinic. Into a conference room they went. I asked them what I could do and asked them if they wanted me to stay. "No thanks," came the reply.

In an hour or two, they asked me back in. What they recommended was brilliant. The team wanted to use a peer-rating system. Each month they voted on whom they, not management, thought was the best employee. The reason—the workers know who works the hardest, not management. They know who is goofing off and who doesn't. The other recommendations included having six separate "Employee of the Month" programs, one for each clinic. They no longer wanted a savings bond. Each team member went back to their clinic and convinced them to buy a plaque so they could put the names of the winners on it for all to see. Finally, they would take the winner out for breakfast.

If management had suggested this idea, it would have generated a plethora of complaints. The new program started resulting in a more fair, motivating program. It empowered the workers, cost me less money, and took less of my time to administer. You can't have it any better than that. General George Patton said, "Never tell people how to do things. Tell them what you want to achieve and they will surprise you with their ingenuity."

Avoiding Workteam Pitfalls

Many companies today find themselves in the middle of a combat situation. They are not facing a foreign enemy from overseas, but a hostile work environment assaulted with rapid change, tougher competition, and rising costs. The innovative leader should consider the strategic advantages of teams and teamwork.

There is a big difference between people working together and working together effectively. The major differences involve how teams make decisions. Teams and teamwork do not fit every situation and every work environment. Many people have difficulty adapting to the team environment and depending on their personality and characteristics, may not be best suited for teamwork.

Team leadership requires a modified form of leadership. The team leader's role requires them to become more like a coach or facilitator rather than a boss. The leader must learn to capitalize on each person's skills, abilities, and differences. They help the team from stumbling into the following pitfalls.

→ Team members jump into solving the problem before accurately defining the problem. They try to solve the symptoms instead of root causes.

→ Team members are not sensitive to individual differences in thinking and problem solving.

→ Teams fail to use a methodology for solving problems.

→ Members fail to develop as a team and undervalue the importance of trust and group cohesion.

→ Members tend to focus on the job instead of focusing on the process and the needs of the customer.

→ Leaders may steer teams toward hidden agendas.

→ Teams and teamwork are not viewed as an important part of the job but rather as an extra duty.

→ Members spend valuable time chasing rabbits and not following the charter.

→ Management does not give teams time for meetings.

→ Management does not provide the team with the right kind of training.

Team Roles and Responsibilities

Other pitfalls can be avoided by keeping the team focused and on track. This involves clear roles and responsibilities.

☞ **Guidance Team/Steering Group.** This group is a senior level organization designed to oversee all teams and projects within the organization. Their main job is to provide the resources that include the training, support, and guidance required during the meeting process. They approve the charter, the timelines, and the final recommendations. They help in clearing obstacles and barriers and monitor progress, keeping the team on track.

☞ **Process Owner/Sponsor.** The process owner is the person who is accountable to the senior executive, president, or CEO of the company. This person owns the actual process the team is chartered to work on. The process owner may also be a member on the team.

☞ **Team Leader.** The team leader is the person who runs the meetings and arranges the various logistical details involved. The team leader orchestrates the meeting process. The team leader works with the process owner/sponsor by establishing the necessary goals and objectives in accordance with the charter.

☞ **Advisor/Facilitator.** This person plays a critical role by helping the team leader, keeping the meeting on-track and focused. The facilitator has the important skills in decision-making techniques, problem solving, and process management methodologies. This person provides training to the other team members as needed.

☞ **Team Members.** These people carry out the various assignments, collect data, and make the improvements. Team members use a project-by-project improvement process.

Project-By-Project Improvement Process

We admire those who have created brand new technologies and inventive products. We like going for the home run, impressed by the new and innovative. But alas, many of us fail to see the mountain of gold waiting at the end of the rainbow. This gold lies at the feet of those who continuously improve upon the normal, everyday business tasks and functions.

Businesses take for granted how the process of work is accomplished. Many managers become experts in fighting fires. They are great in solving whatever pops up, instead of managing strategically. Managing strategically means taking a project-by-project improvement strategy. By taking a project-by-project approach, businesses can make revolutionary improvements. When working with teams, the project-by-project improvement strategy involves an 11-step process.

1. **Identify projects.** Search your business for areas needing improvement. Look for projects by asking your customers, your managers, your employees. Gather information from customer surveys.

2. **Select a project.** Pick the project with the greatest return on your investment.

3. **Form a team.** Put together the right team with the right members. Membership comes from all areas of the organization represented in the project.

4. **Establish a charter.** Agree on the purpose of the team and the team goal, and write out a mission statement (see the sample charter in this chapter).

5. **Analyze the project.** Identify possible root causes and begin identifying solutions.

6. **Design solutions.** Allow the team to analyze each possible solution in detail. Bring in subject matter experts to provide advice and special information surrounding the project.

7. **Test the solutions.** Do a partial application to insure the solutions will remedy the problem.

8. **Implement.** Complete an implementation plan involving those affected by the change. Insure the plan includes the how, when, and where, as it impacts on the remedy.

9. **Measure the results.** Monitor the changes to insure it is working as planned. Make adjustments and continue to monitor and measure the results.

10. **Celebrate Success.** Create a celebration for those members who participated on the team.

11. **Nominate new projects.** Start over again, solving and improving all projects/problems.

Team Charters

When working with teams, the smallest detail can have major consequences. A charter is a tool used to clarify the purpose and mission of the team. It forms a bridge between the steering group and the team. It lays out expectations and can help the team avoid spending time working on unnecessary details unrelated to the project.

SAMPLE TEAM CHARTER

1. Purpose: To decrease the amount of time it takes to fulfill telephone orders from customers. (The purpose must be clear and succinct. It should use active verb statements, such as decrease, reduce, improve, decide, etc.)

2. Mission: To assemble a process action team to study the present situation and decide the best course of action. (Further clarify the goal of the team).

3. Expected Improvements:

    a. Identifying improvements that enhance the relationship between this organization and our customers.

    b. Developing a faster way to fulfill telephone orders.

    c. Creating a more efficient, effective, and responsive organization tailored to the customers' needs and expectations.

4. Expected Outcomes:

    a. Assemble a process action team with the following members:

        Office: John Doe   Office: Jane Doe

        Office: John Doe   Office: Jane Doe

        Office: Jane Doe   Office: John Doe

    b. Prepare a transition plan with a timeline to accomplish recommendations.

    c. Remove barriers and obstacles. The PAT is empowered to challenge existing constraints. Do not be constrained by internal restrictions, policies, and procedures or current organization hierarchy.

  d. Decide meeting frequency (responsibility of the PAT).

  e. Solicit customers and suppliers as advisors when needed.

5. Authority:

  a. Process owner: Mary Doe.

  b. Team leader: John F. Smudge.

  c. Team facilitator: Jane S. Doe.

6. Boundaries and Reporting Requirements:

  a. The PAT will become active on January 18, 1996 and will remain active by Sept. 30, 1996 or until relieved by the Executive Steering Council.

  b. It should be prepared to provide the ESC an In Progress Review (IPR) on March 10th.

  c. All tasks and milestones included in the approved transition plan and timelines are to be achieved by Sept. 30, 1996. If needed, extensions will be provided by the ESC.

(Signature)_____   _____

ESC Chairperson   Process Owner

_____   _____

Team Leader   Facilitator

CHAPTER 10

INNOVATION: A NEW DEFINITION FOR NEW TIMES

"Good artists imitate, great artists steal."

—Pablo Picasso

Walt Disney once said, "In this volatile business of ours we can ill afford to rest on our laurels, even to pause in retrospect. Times and conditions change so rapidly that we must keep our aim constantly on the future." As mentioned in another chapter, many businesses are in trouble today because they were sleeping at the wheel. American businesses failed to see the competitive challenges happening oversees as well as within our own borders, until it was almost too late.

One morning America woke up to discover foreign imports sitting in every other driveway. Look at Sears, IBM, RCA, buggy whips, carbon paper, typewriters, and LP phono records. All around we see painful reminders of those products and businesses that lost sight of what was happening around them. Many businesses learned a valuable lesson, but many others remain clueless. They fail to recognize the importance of innovation, as well as how to create an innovative environment.

The nation as a whole has come along way. We've become more competitive and still rank as the most productive nation in the world. However, no matter how confident we feel today, success is only temporary—here today and gone tomorrow. All organizations must stand vigilant and be ever mindful of Walt Disney's words, "...we can ill afford to rest on our laurels...we must keep our aim constantly on the future."

Innovation and creativity are no longer optional, but the key for survival for all organizations. Innovation is not reserved for those organizations and those people who work in Silicon Valley or those who make six-figure incomes. Innovation is not just the job of brilliant scientists. Some of the greatest ideas and the best innovators are front-line workers. They are truck drivers, parents at PTA meetings, school children, citizens at the voting polls—those people closest to the problem. People have tremendous ideas, but most organizations don't understand the process for capturing, nurturing, and transforming ideas into usable and profitable commodities.

Creating an innovative environment is a nonstop operation. Innovation is a process, a science, one critical for success in all

businesses, in all organizations. The way we manage our businesses, our schools, and our governments today may be the very thing that gets us in trouble tomorrow, leading to disaster. More important today than ever before, leaders—men and women—are needed who can chart a new course, who understand the innovation process and can lead their businesses to new islands of opportunity.

What is Innovation?

The world as we know it was built upon the innovative ideas of people. These innovative ideas have blossomed into businesses and products revolutionizing the way we live and work. Images come to mind of people like Thomas Edison, Walt Disney, Bill Gates, Anita Roddick, and even Larry Harmon, owner of the De Mar Air-Conditioning and Plumbing Company in Clovis, California.

Innovation means many things to many people, but it boils down to just to one key element. It means taking an idea and transforming it into reality. It doesn't have to be an original idea either. Innovation can be either a brand new idea or the application of an old idea to a new technology, a new product or a new service.

Innovation, Creativity, and the Plumbing Business

What image comes to mind when you think of a plumber? Whatever the image is, here is a plumbing company that gives that image a total makeover. Have you ever heard of a plumbing company that sends its technicians ("service advisors") to Dale Carnegie training, provides gift certificates, or send technicians to customers on time? These are only a few of the many innovations Larry Harmon, President of De Mar Plumbing Company, has incorporated into his magic toolbox.

Like a thousand points of light, there is nothing ordinary about this Clovis, California company. From it's bright yellow and red service trucks with $2,400 paint jobs, its gift certificates, and the special awards and recognition provided for his service advisors, this company breaks all rules and plows new ground. Not only do they make the customer happy, but they make a lot of money. In six years, they went from $210,000 to $4 million in sales—six times the national average. Whatever they're doing—it works.

Old Way—New Way

From beginning to end, De Mar stands out from the pack because of their emphasis on customer service. Larry Harmon has a simple but powerful philosophy. He says, "People buy two things: solutions to problems and good feelings.... Solving problems is what they pay us to do...but where we go above and beyond that is making sure they have good feelings about our company."

I admire any company who spends the time to ask customers what they want, and then turns around and gives them even more than they ask for.

→ **Same Day Service**—The number one customer complaint in the service industry is, "They never show up when they say they will." De Mar completes all service appointments the same day they are called in. Service advisors don't go home until they complete all appointments.

→ **Price Guarantee**—De Mar quotes the price of all work before they begin. Customers are charged by the job, not by the hour. If the advisor underprices the job, De Mar pays the difference, not the customer.

→ **Round-the-Clock Service**—Air conditioners and plumbing problems never happen at convenient times and when they break, it is an emergency to the customer. Uniformed advisors come to your home or place of business, repair the item, and charge the same price, regardless of the hour. Service advisors get overtime pay for after-hours service; however, the cost of overtime is offset by loyal customers and repeat business. Word-of-mouth advertising has been De Mar's best form of marketing.

➔ **Gift Certificates/Senior Citizen Discounts**—How would you like a De Mar gift certificate for your birthday? Both of these programs transform the ordinary into the extraordinary—novel ideas bringing in new business.

➔ **Preferred Customer Discount Club**—Customers get their own distinctive red and yellow wallet card. The card entitles preferred customers to a 10 percent discount off all labor performed by any De Mar service advisor. Senior citizens receive an additional 5 percent discount. The name of the service advisor also goes on the card, and he receives an extra 2 percent commission on the total bill. Harmon says he got that idea from AmWay.

➔ **Great Guarantees**—If any of their work should fail within 12 months, they promise to fix it at no charge, 100 percent guaranteed.

➔ **Training and Development**—Each year approximately 2 percent of De Mar's gross revenues go to employee training and development. In addition to their $15,000 video and tape library, service advisors attend a 12-week Dale Carnegie course costing $20,000 per employee.

➔ **Employee Incentives**—De Mar is not a cake ride. Service advisors work longer and harder than most. The dispatcher is on call 24 hours a day. Advisors occasionally work anywhere from 8 to 16-hour days. Longer hours are common during peak seasons. Their hard work and exceptional service is rewarded based on a point system. Advisors get 250 points for a positive phone call from a customer. A letter of appreciation is worth 500 points. For a customer to ask for a specific advisor is worth a whopping 3,000 points, and on it goes, including deductions for mistakes.

➔ **Pay for Performance**—The top three service advisors receive a 50 percent pay raise during the next pay period. A $50 weekly bonus comes to the person who has the best idea for improving customer service. This point system helped one service advisor make $65,000 a couple of years ago.

Larry Harmon has given new meaning to the saying, "Build it and they will come." In his own words, he explains his success formula for his exceptional growth: "We just kind of figured if we gave good service, the growth would take care of itself." He concludes by saying, "Have a Deee-marvelous day!"

A Tale of Two Organizations

Success in the past depended on many factors, including autocratic command and control, economy of scale, and being able to out-produce the competition. Margaret Wheatly, author of *Management and the New Science*, says many business organizations resemble fortresses more than anything else. This is the environment many people face every day when arriving at the office door. Success in the new millennium depends on an entirely new set of factors.

Innovation Explained

An Innovative enterprise does the following:

- ☞ **Continually listens to and looks at new ways of doing things,**

- ☞ **Improves and refines existing services and products,**

- ☞ **Improves internal processes and systems allowing the organization to stay successful, and**

- ☞ **Exceeds customer expectations.**

An Innovative enterprise also does the following:

- ☞ **Creates work environments that encourage people to take risks and use their initiative,**

☛ **Removes barriers and obstacles so people take pride in their work,**

☛ **Allows people to have access to each other no matter the rank or position,**

☛ **Provides everyone information on the plans and goals of the organization, and**

☛ **Maintains these qualities over time.**

An Innovative enterprise has leaders who:

☛ **Are not threatened by change,**

☛ **Create a charged environment that motivates people to reach their potential,**

☛ **Support innovative ideas and suggestions, and**

☛ **Create pathways of communication to facilitate, sponsor, and protect innovative ideas and suggestions.**

Innovative enterprises do not have to:

☛ **Create every new idea—instead, spend time looking at and studying good ideas from outside the organization.**

☛ **Create a brand new product or tool—that's invention.**

☛ **Simply come up with new ideas—that's creativity.**

There are two basic types of organizations: the innovative enterprise and the traditional type of organization. The difference between the two has little to do with size, structure, or the type of industry. What matters is the environment, the leadership, and the ability within the organization to innovate.

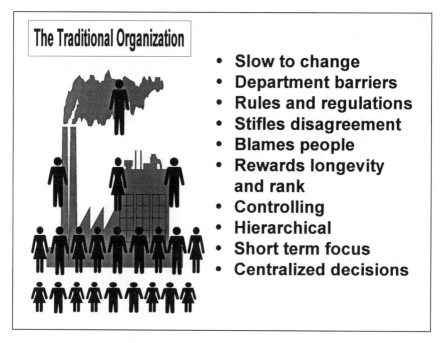

The Traditional Organization

- **Slow to change**
- **Department barriers**
- **Rules and regulations**
- **Stifles disagreement**
- **Blames people**
- **Rewards longevity and rank**
- **Controlling**
- **Hierarchical**
- **Short term focus**
- **Centralized decisions**

Traditional Troubles

The traditional organization must adapt to the changing environment. It makes decisions slowly and reactively, losses focus, and becomes out of touch with those it serves. Because of these factors, it sometimes makes bad decisions. The traditional organization provides limited information and communication to the workers. Often workers must depend on the rumor mill and other ineffective forms of communication to find out what's happening. Finance finds it increasingly difficult to talk to Marketing. Sales doesn't know what Research and Development is doing, and senior management "never lets anyone know what's going on."

Occasionally, people try to raise innovative ideas. They try to push them up the organizational ladder to the decision makers. Many times the ideas mature, but the majority hit a wall of molasses never to flower. After a while, people quit trying, further adding to their disenchantment. We've allowed the system to make decisions, and sad to say, initiative is looking more and more like inertia. Citizens, customers, workers—all walks of people feel

The Innovative Organization

- **Empowered workers**
- **Continuous learning**
- **Allows risk taking**
- **Ideas more than rank**
- **Long-range view**
- **Everyone involved**
- **Ownership**
- **"We" not "they"**
- **Trained and motivated**
- **Values teamwork**
- **Rewards and recognition**

a growing frustration, and anger is beginning to stalk the hallways of many of our institutions.

As described earlier in this book, innovation is built on a framework of three key elements—Accessibility, Information, and Motivation. These three keys help to transform the traditional way of managing to a more innovative one. Leadership remains as the guiding force making this formula successful.

A Greater Calling

Creating the innovative environment is easier when it becomes part of the overall business strategy. For several years I ran the Office of Innovation and Total Quality Management for the Army Medical Department. In the late 1980s, several federal agencies and military organizations joined to create the Federal Healthcare Network. Senior medical officials, including the Surgeon Generals from the Army, Air Force, Navy, Veterans Administration, and Public Health Service signed a proclamation forming the Federal Healthcare Innovation Network. Their task was to work toward "providing high quality and efficient healthcare services to all beneficiaries."

These services realized it was much more efficient to combine their ideas and resources than to work separately. They had set for themselves several goals:

→ To heighten awareness of the need for creative ideas from all people throughout the federal healthcare organization.

→ To create an organizational climate that recognizes failure as an integral part of the "growth cycle" and welcomes change as opportunity.

→ To constantly pursue creative, innovative, and alternative methodologies to meet the challenges of a constantly changing healthcare delivery system.

→ To communicate top management's commitment to encouraging and rewarding those who make innovative contributions.

Steps Toward Successful Innovation

Generating ideas is the first step in the innovation process. Getting people to give ideas is easier than implementing those ideas. Taking those ideas and creating new products and services is a war won or lost in the trenches of the innovation process. Someone once said innovation is 3 percent inspiration and 97 percent perspiration. Innovation is hard work, and it is particularly harder for larger organizations. Successful innovation is the result of the following steps:

STEP 1   CREATE THE RIGHT ENVIRON-
MENT.

As was stressed previously in this book, one of the most important jobs of the manager is to create a leadership environment. Leaders are in many respects environmentalists. Leaders create either a positive or negative work environment. The leader challenges the status quo, removes barriers, provides information, and provides training and rewards that encourage risk taking. These elements form a critical bond by creating the right environment, helping foster new ideas and innovation.

People are born with natural creative abilities. They have ideas. Particularly important to note, it is the workers, not management, who usually have the best ideas. The workers have the answers to management's problems because they are the ones closest to reality—the front-line. We all must learn to become more receptive to new ideas. After listening to someone's idea, the first words out of our mouths will either encourage or discourage.

Phrases Damaging the Environment

We know everything already.

Let's think about this before we invest any money.

No one has tried that before.

That idea won't necessarily help this department that much.

We haven't budgeted for that this year.

We've already tried that before, and it didn't work out.

Let's get a few other opinions first.

Where's the data to support this?

Let's talk about it in the next staff meeting.

I don't think it would work here!

You gotta be kidding?

Things are different here.

Let's staff it around the office.

That's a good idea, but...

I think there is a rule that says we can't do that.

Well, you haven't been here as long as the others.

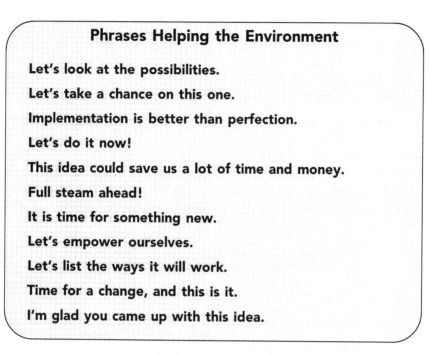

Phrases Helping the Environment

Let's look at the possibilities.

Let's take a chance on this one.

Implementation is better than perfection.

Let's do it now!

This idea could save us a lot of time and money.

Full steam ahead!

It is time for something new.

Let's empower ourselves.

Let's list the ways it will work.

Time for a change, and this is it.

I'm glad you came up with this idea.

STEP 2   UNDERSTAND THE PROCESS OF INNOVATION

The process of innovation has been described as a relay race with many hand-offs. Any time the baton drops, innovation ceases.

Americans lead the world with their ideas, inventions, and entrepreneurial pursuits. However, Americans have difficulty transforming and implementing innovative ideas into usable products and services. Instead of taking an idea from beginning to end, it appears we would rather invent a new product or start a new business. American style management focuses on the one "big idea." Instead of small and incremental improvements, we try to hit the "home run." This approach occasionally gets us into trouble with our competitors.

Unlike Western management, Asian cultures unify their efforts and are better at developing, implementing, and improving innovative ideas and processes. For example, during the design process, Japanese businesses involve as many people as possible. They study every aspect of the product, incorporating important features. Once the product goes into production, it has reached a high level of thoroughness, detail, and design competence. Although this is a laborious process, the final product is more likely to be enthusiastically implemented, supported, and carried out with fewer errors and delays.

Types of Innovation

There are two types of innovation: evolutionary and revolutionary. Evolutionary innovation or process innovation is the mechanism of continuously improving a product or service. Take, for example, the Sony Corporation continuously adding new features with every model of the Sony Walkman. Look at the Ford Taurus—each year it has included new features, making it one of the best-selling automobiles in the world. Recently, the Ford Taurus was completely redesigned.

The other type of innovation is revolutionary innovation. The Post-It note from 3M is a revolutionary idea. The CD laser disk is another example of revolutionary innovation. Innovation isn't just the domain of high-technology industries, but applies to all aspects of business life and all types of businesses.

Innovation Process

Innovation is surrounded by much confusion and fuzziness. There are many words sometimes mistakenly used yet associated with innovation. For the sake of clarity, let's define a few important words:

→ **Creativity:** The environment from which people create ideas.

→ **Innovation:** The hard work associated with transforming ideas into usable products and services. Robert Rosenfield says innovation is taking ideas and "making money with them."

→ **Process:** A series of related steps within the transformation process.

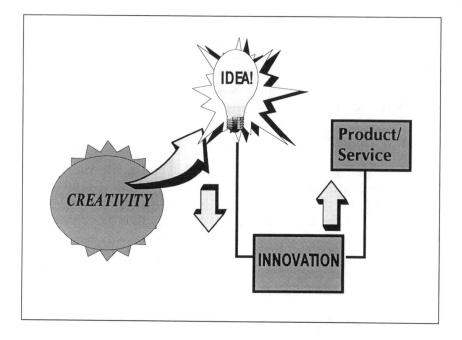

Success Stories

Here are a few other organizations that have successfully applied the innovative process.

National Bank

The National Bank of Detroit offered their customers $10 every time they found an error in their bank statements. This new way of doing business brought in 15,000 new accounts and over $65.5 million in new business in the first two months.

Police Department

In the 1980s the Reno, Nevada Police Department faced a rising vehicle accident rate. So with typical police department mentality, the Reno police doubled the number of traffic citations and bought an additional 21 radar units. Guess what—the accident rate didn't drop, and the community became angry with the police. So the police tried something different.

Taking a few ideas from the Harrah's Casino Hotel, the police started asking citizens for their advice on how to lower the accident rate. The police department started surveying the citizens by telephone. Because of the survey, police pinpointed the root causes and the problems contributing to vehicle accidents. By changing dangerous intersections, adjusting speed limits, and using speed-monitoring signs, the accident rate dropped 20 percent during the first six months.

Clothing Store

Mansour's, a clothing store in Columbus, Georgia, identified an innovative opportunity during the holiday season. They ship any item purchased by customers to any location in the United States free. How convenient—they simplified the shopping process, saving customers time and effort. You can send something to relatives or friends without having to box it, wrap it, take it to the post office, weigh it, insure it, and finally mail it. Mansour's succeeds where other "normal" clothing stores fail because of this innovative customer service program.

STEP 3   FOCUS ON THE TARGET OF INNOVATION

Organizations can enhance their innovative efforts by clearly targeting their particular areas of interest. In other words, management must say, "These are the areas we are most interested in. What can we do?"

You never want to discourage people's ideas, but focusing and prioritizing saves time and resources. Separating the gold nuggets from the diamonds is the job of the leader. Guidance is provided by the vision statement, goals, and objectives. Another way to focus is doing a market analysis including the trends, environmental changes, and problems customers are experiencing. A **partial market analysis** can be completed by asking these questions:

→ **What new products or services can we create?**

→ **What areas of status quo can we improve in our organization?**

→ **What new management approaches would improve our operations?**

→ **What are the threats to our industry?**

→ **What problems keep coming up over and over again?**

→ **What are our customers saying about our company?**

→ **What do outside experts and consultants say about us?**

→ **What are our competitors doing?**

→ **What areas can we speed up or eliminate?**

STEP 4   DEVELOP A SYSTEM TO CAPTURE AND TRANSFORM IDEAS

This is one of the most important steps in the entire process. All leaders mean well and want to make a positive difference. Often the enthusiasm to make a difference interferes with the "process" of making a difference. Innovation requires a system.

There are few more damaging actions than asking for people's ideas and then not doing or being able to do anything with those ideas. Many times we can get in trouble by putting the cart before the horse. We must build the foundation of innovation before asking for ideas. What is needed is a system that captures the ideas, and supports, nurtures, and analyzes those ideas until they can be implemented and applied to the business. Here is a system to help build your innovative environment.

→ **Dig for Ideas**—If you want innovation, you must ask for it. Spend the energy to create programs and ways to search out ideas. The next chapter goes into more detail on how to do this.

→ **Appoint Idea/Quality Coaches**—Assign or appoint people to serve as coaches or internal consultants in

HOW TO KILL INNOVATION

- **Negative attitude toward ideas that come from below**
- **Too many approval levels**
- **Traditional recognition**
- **Secret and numerous changes**
- **Micro management**
- **"We know everything" attitude**
- **"I think, you do!" attitude**
- **"Do as I say, not as I do"**

each office or department. They become an interdepartmental resource linking their department's ideas, concerns, and training needs with the organizational innovation office. They receive special training in process facilitation, quality, and innovation.

→ **Take it to the Innovation Office**—The Innovation Office serves as the gatekeeper for all ideas requiring coordination. This office, staffed full-time or by people detailed from other offices, provides the conduit for ideas up and down the organizational ladder.

→ **Find a Champion**—Charles Kettering once said, "If you want to kill any idea in the world, get a committee working on it." Good ideas die an early death unless they are nurtured and supported. The champion is a person who believes in, devotes time to, and is willing to pursue ideas aggressively. The champion, along with the sponsor, helps cut through the red tape and across all boundaries, until the idea comes to fruition.

→ **Connect with a Sponsor**—A sponsor is usually a senior ranking person who has the resources, ownership,
and power to support the idea. This person, along with
the champion, helps in clearing away obstacles to
insure the complete development and transformation
of the idea into a usable product or service.

Innovative: Ordinary to Extraordinary

Hardware Store

An example of an ordinary business transforming itself into an
extraordinary business is Highland Hardware located in Atlanta,
Georgia. What can be extraordinary about a hardware store? Well,
this hardware store not only carries the traditional screws, washers,
and PVC pipe, but has an innovative difference.

Highland Hardware's caters to the woodworker. Their shelves
are stocked with a wide variety of tools, equipment, and wood-
working products. They have dozens of saws. They have all types
of drills. Hundreds of furniture plans and books beckon people who
love making saw dust. One of the most significant differences
about Highland Hardware is their catalog business. Catalog sales
have generated an additional 60 percent for their business.

A recent expansion project added a classroom for seminars
and workshops. Chris Bagby, the owner, invites famous woodwork-
ers to come teach at the Highland Hardware. The last time I went
shopping at Highland Hardware, mobs of people were buying all
types of items. All these innovative differences have helped to
double their business during the past 10 years. With the right kind
of leadership, ordinary quickly becomes extraordinary.

Restaurant

Porky's Restaurant is located in Gulf Shores, Alabama. I stopped
there once to use the telephone. I was so impressed, I stayed to have
breakfast. Each booth in the restaurant has it's own television set
built right into the wall. In addition to the TVs, there is a telephone
at each table. They provide free local calls and free long distance

calls after 5 P.M. when you buy your meal. I watched a man at a booth make call after call to his business associates while he ate his meal. Lots of vacationers came here to catch up with the news and make calls back home. The restaurant was booming. Who would ever think to put televisions and free telephones at a restaurant?

Hospital

Noble Army Community Hospital, Fort McClellan, Alabama, implemented a program that not only increased patient satisfaction but also elevated the quality level of health care. Each day the staff randomly calls selected patients seen at the hospital during the previous day. They ask two questions: (1) "Are you feeling better?" and (2) "What did you like about your visit?" Then the patient is given the opportunity to tell how the hospital can improve its services.

This program produced many benefits. Patients are pleased that the hospital shows enough concern to call them and ask about their welfare. They feel more trusting of the hospital. The staff gains information, ideas, and suggestions for improvement.

The results and comments from the patients are tabulated and put into a report. The report is circulated throughout the hospital. This gives the clinics specific feedback on what needs improving and what pleases the patients most. The report eventually returns to the Medical Staff Executive Committee. The committee now has real-time information on patient satisfaction and trends.

Summary

There are several important points to remember.

→ **All organizations must become more innovative or face extinction.**

→ **All people are naturally creative and have great ideas.**

→ **Ideas are the lifeblood of productive organizations.**

→ **Organizations should develop a system of capturing and transforming ideas into usable products or services.**

→ **Innovation transforms an ordinary service or product into something extraordinary.**

→ **The job of management is to create an innovative work environment.**

CHAPTER 11

THE GOLD MINE IN PEOPLE'S IDEAS

"New ideas are always suspect, and usually opposed, without any other reason than because they are not already common."

—John Locke

I graduated from North Georgia College, which lies at the feet of the Blue Ridge Mountains in Dahlonega, Georgia. In the 1800s, Dahlonega was the site of one of the largest gold rushes in American history. On weekends I went to the rivers to pan for gold. I would hike the mountains and explored old mines of the previous century. In my mind, I saw those miners and felt their excitement as they, picks in hand, chipped away, searching for gold. I hoped to strike it rich and to find a vein of gold somewhere under the surface. My explorations never revealed much gold, but I learned some valuable lessons worth more than anything I uncovered within the ground.

Businesses need gold miners—people who chip away at the crust of bureaucracy and stagnation to discover real gold in people's ideas, their natural creativity. Unfortunately, in many places we've substituted the process of innovation and creativity with structured rank and file, committees, and special task forces. We've certified and credentialed people to the point where initials behind a name and the rank on a collar are more significant than one's ability to produce results. The highest concern of people at the top of the pyramid should be, "Who has the best ideas and how can we get them?"

The Front-Line Speaks Out!

I've been teaching leadership courses for many years. The people who attended my classes and seminars represent all collars—blue-collar, white-collar, and gold-collar workers. They are from the service, technology, government, and manufacturing industries. Business owners and executives, as well as front-line workers, all come to learn more about innovation and leadership. At the end of each session, I ask them two important questions:

1. "What motivates you to come to work?"

2. "Are you reaching your potential on the job?"

In all cases, the answers follow a similar pattern. Of the two questions, the answer to the second question disturbed me the most. Shockingly, 70 percent said "no." They were not reaching their potential. They felt they could be contributing more to the job.

The answer to the first question was more revealing. To discover what motivated them at work, I gave each person a ten-item list and asked them to rate each item as to how it motivated them at work. They were asked to rate each item on a scale from 1–10, number 1 being the most important and number 10 being the least. On a scale of 1-10, these are the results of the survey.

1. Ability to contribute to the business

2. Challenging job opportunities

3. Supportive supervisors

4. Recognition for a job well done

5. Promotion opportunities

6. Pay/salary

7. Educational opportunities

8. Medical benefits

9. Flex time

10. Retirement benefits

Bridging the Potential Gap

There were some individual differences based on age and seniority, but the results of this survey were clear. People gained the greatest amount of motivation from challenging job opportunities and the ability to contribute to the business. I had expected pay/salary to be one of the top motivators. Money is important to people, but is not as motivational as the others.

The best way to tap the potential and improve the motivation of people is to create an environment that allows them to contribute to the job. This environment comes from a variety of ways. People feel they are contributing to the business when someone listens to and implements their ideas. The purpose of this chapter is to show how to capture the ideas of people. Managers and leaders who can create this empowering environment will be the winners in the twenty-first century.

The Japanese Way

We are aware of the legendary performance in Japanese companies. In the typical 1,000-person Japanese company, 778 people submit 25,328 new ideas and suggestions. In a typical American company of the same size, only 90 people submit ideas in which fewer than 35 are implemented. Why is there such a big difference?

The idea rich process typical in many Japanese companies didn't happen overnight. It evolved over years with many changes and improvements. Like all dynamic systems, it continues to evolve.

Survival always provides an incentive for change. You only have to stub your toe once to learn to pick up your feet. In the 1950s and 1960s, Japanese workers averaged less than one suggestion per year. The traditional Japanese culture inhibited individual thinking. Individuals were not encouraged to come up with ideas. The group was more important than the individual. The devastation during the war and the oil crisis in the 1970s forced the Japanese people and businesses into finding better ways of working. They realized that the old way was not going to bring success, so they started changing, and as with most change, it didn't come easy.

Today, like many American businesses, the Japanese made a complete transformation. During the past 30 years, they have created a culture where the workers constantly improve what they do. They have taken the suggestion program or the idea process and refined it into an art. The Japanese word for this is *Kaizen* or continuous improvement. For example, in 1979, Hitachi generated 2.29 million suggestions in one year. Kaizen provides them a strength that catapults them competitively ahead of businesses around the world.

The point cannot be any clearer. Any company focusing on continuous improvement holds the key to greatness and competitive superiority. Constant idea generation and constant innovation will put any business ahead of the pack. The key to greatness begins with creating a culture where people automatically generate innovative ideas and a management structure that is willing to implement them.

The Trouble with Employee Involvement Programs

There is nothing wrong with employee involvement programs or management philosophies. What is wrong is the method in which they are carried out. Most programs take a top-down, "sheep dip" approach, a "program mentality." Management tries to baptize people with the new program from the top down. Send them to a two-hour class, buy the new book, and bring in the expert. The trouble with most employee involvement programs is that they follow these steps:

IMPLEMENTATION PLAN

Step 1—Appoint a special commission/committee

Step 2—Spend lots of money

Step 3—Expend lots of enthusiasm

Step 4—Discover disillusionment

Step 5—Search for the results

Step 6—Panic

Step 7—Punish the innocent

Step 8—Provide rewards and honors for non-participants

Step 9—Revert back to the old way

In general terms, typical employee involvement programs are like going on a diet. There is a lot of enthusiasm in the beginning. As time goes on and weight loss slows down, people quit the diet. In the business world, TQM, reengineering, and other philosophies, tools, and techniques focus on changing the organizational culture. Changing an organization's management culture takes both a long time and a lot of energy.

Executives spend valuable time coming up with vision statements, goals, and strategic plans. New posters go on the walls. Keynote speakers come in and all the while, managers are trying to keep the business running. Management wants results. Frontline workers want changes. Somewhere along the journey, they all get lost and frustrated. Like Alice in Wonderland, the organization gives up the "new way" and returns to the "old way" of doing business.

Without results and improvements, people will claim that TQM, or whatever the program is, doesn't work—"I told you so." Then here comes the negative publicity by the well-meaning but mis-guided media claiming another failure. Management jumps on the next fad or technique repeating the sad cycle all over again. Meanwhile, workers and management are becoming more reluc-tant to try anything new—no matter the benefits. Consultants and managers both share in the blame. Sadly, most managers and many consultants don't know how to manage for change.

For lack of a better definition, I will call the new employee involvement program, the "new way." The new way must be implemented by using both a top-down, and most importantly, a bottom-up approach. The bottom-up approach is the one we will cover thoroughly below.

Bottom-Up Approach to Change

Peter Drucker in his book, *Managing in Turbulent Times,* said, "One has to assume, first, that the individual human being at work knows better than anyone else what makes him or her more productive—even in routine work, the only true expert is the per-son who does the job." Getting employees' ideas and getting their involvement is not an option anymore. If we are going to remain competitive, it's mandatory we involve the workers in the process. The right way depends on what the strategy or concept is and how the new way is implemented.

There are two specific reasons why employee involvement pro-grams and new management philosophies fail. Each of the rea-sons relates to the other. First, there is a considerable lag time between the initial classes, meetings, etc., and the actual results. Because organizations use a top-down process, it takes weeks or months before any significant changes occur. In the mean time, the workers and middle management get frustrated and lose inter-est. One writer suggests that, "...while managers pour time and resources into total quality, and fall further behind waiting for the results, a vast reservoir of untapped and unsuspected capacity remains concealed in the work force." Lag time can be shortened or eliminated all together.

The second reason for failure stems from the fact that the worker is usually left out of the change process. While managers are up in the stratosphere working on strategic visioning processes, values, and merger strategies, the average worker is dealing with everyday reality. Reality is full of problems.

Day in and day out, workers face the same frustrating problems. "The bathroom faucet won't turn off...We can't get copy paper from the supply room...Customers hate voice mail, no one ever returns their calls...The software program won't work the way it is supposed to" and on and on. Unless management adjusts its focus to help solve the workers' problems, the workers are not going to be interested in helping management with its problems.

The front-line worker has the solutions to most of management's problems. Most people want to contribute to their job, want to make a positive difference. An organization reaps many rewards by focusing on the front-line, capturing workers' ideas, and solving their problems.

As we said above, the trouble with most performance improvement programs is their failure to generate results early on, leaving the front-line worker out of the process. Management must avoid the "sheep dip" approach or "program mentality" to employee involvement. Employees become much more motivated when they see their issues resolved or their ideas implemented. Results get people excited and ready for the long haul, leading to a total organizational transformation. To get people excited about change and involved, we must create an enthusiastic, zestful environment.

The Zest Factor

How many times have you asked employees for their ideas and suggestions and got nothing more than blank stares and shrugged shoulders? Are the only things you find in your suggestion boxes trash and cobwebs? Don't feel alone—this is normal for most American businesses.

It is not as much a reflection of the worker as it is how we go about asking. Most typical suggestion programs spell—BORING! Not only are suggestion programs boring, but the entire work environment is boring. To get things going, people and businesses need a shot in the arm. Businesses don't have to spend tremendous amounts of money and a lengthy cycle of training and change management to do this. It be done with only a small investment of time and money.

Work can be fun, exciting, and challenging. It sometimes takes a crisis to capture the enthusiasm and creativity of the workforce. This does not have to be a crisis in the negative sense, but a crisis in the positive sense. During a crisis, performance peaks. Creativity, imagination, and innovation are the by-products of crisis management. A short-term crisis based on urgency, excitement, and fun gets workers excited, helping them reach their potential. This is called the Zest Factor.

Robert Schaffer, in a *New York Times* article, identified four "zest factors" that create high energy and motivation. They were:

→ **A clear and compelling goal,**

→ **Success within reasonable grasp,**

→ **A collaborate mode, and**

→ **A genuine sense of fun and excitement.**

By understanding the zest factor, we stand a better chance of implementing our programs and philosophies with success. A zestful environment comes by creating a crisis.

Getting Gassed: The Power of Crisis Management

As a young Second Lieutenant in the Army, I believed in tough, realistic training. I took my platoon to the field for gas-attack training. Along with my other equipment, I obtained several smoke and teargas grenades to take with me to the field. The teargas grenades would add a touch of realism during the training. I soon found out it was more realism than I expected.

The goal of the maneuver was to make my soldiers more confident in the use of their protective masks. One night after warning my soldiers to be on the look out for a possible "gas" attack, I snuck out to surprise them.

I stuffed a bunch of grenades in my pockets. By carefully putting the tear gas grenade in a special pocket, I was sure it wouldn't get mixed up with the smoke grenades. As I snuck up to my platoon, I grabbed a "smoke" grenade. I pulled the pin and tossed it toward my unwary soldiers. Someone yelled, "Gas!" and all my soldiers dutifully put on their protective masks. All did except me, that is, because I knew it was only smoke—so I thought.

So there I was standing in the center of what I thought was a thick cloud of harmless smoke. The next few moments have been forever painfully burned into my memory. I took a deep breath. My eyes burned. I started hacking and gaging. How could this be? I had "gassed" myself!

Instead of throwing the smoke grenade, I had thrown the tear gas grenade by mistake. Now I was the only one in the outfit without a mask on. In milliseconds I sprung up and yanked out my mask, placing it over my face and breaking all performance records.

Besides the obvious one, there is another point to this story. All of us know how a crisis can create a high level of performance. Almost anyone who has experienced a crisis knows how performance, creativity, and innovation improves. Short-term performance increases with the flow of adrenaline. Remember cramming for exams and changing that flat tire? When the crisis ends, performance returns to normal. How does this apply business?

Idea Programs: Making Work Fun

Organized systems must exist that simultaneously capture the potential, fix the problems, and involve the workers. This is done through the use of idea programs. They have been around in various shapes and fashions for over 100 years. Ideas programs run the gamut of hot to cold, everything from the traditional suggestion box to the powerful idea campaigns. Included in this chapter are a couple of specialized idea programs from a few well known organizations.

This section of the chapter outlines different programs, beginning with simple ones and moving to more involved ones. Before actually covering the specific types of programs, here are the **advantages of using idea programs**:

→ Creates ownership and trust within the organization.

→ Improves individual motivation and morale of the workforce.

→ Allows departments and individuals to work cross-functionally.

→ Facilitates change because people share their ideas and are more willing to change.

→ Creates an environment of learning and constant renewal.

→ Improves work methods and processes continually.

→ Reduces costs of doing business.

→ Improves safety and reduces accidents.

→ Empowers the workforce itself, versus waiting for decisions from above.

→ Reduces the we/they syndrome.

→ Improves communication within the organization.

→ Improves employee attitudes.

SUGGESTION BOX

This is probably the most basic of all idea programs. Workers provide suggestions using either a special form or piece of paper. Suggestion box systems are usually slow and haphazardly managed. Suggestion approval suffers from arbitrary decisions by

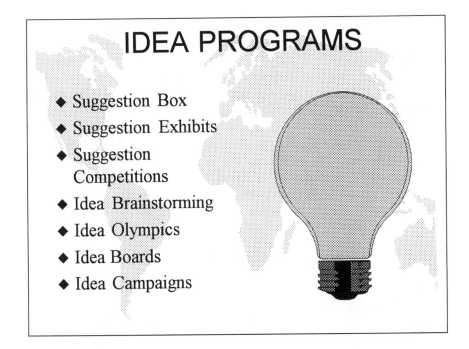

IDEA PROGRAMS

- Suggestion Box
- Suggestion Exhibits
- Suggestion Competitions
- Idea Brainstorming
- Idea Olympics
- Idea Boards
- Idea Campaigns

managers who may be far removed from the idea or problem. The greatest hindrance with suggestion boxes is not the concept, but how the concept is managed. The power of a suggestion box is enhanced by a quick and objective response.

SUGGESTION EXHIBITS

This is a program where people of an organization bring their suggestions, ideas, and new inventions for all to see. This is like an adult show-and-tell process. This program is more exciting and more effective than suggestion boxes. The organization provides a display area and provides a time period for this purpose. It is more readily used in a manufacturing or technical-oriented company; however, it has merit for service industries. It is also a great way to increase networking and improve communication within any enterprise.

SUGGESTION COMPETITIONS

This is a more involved program designed to encourage friendly competition between departments. Management asks departments to make suggestions. The number of suggestions are tabulated and posted each week or month on a wall chart in a public area. What is reported is the number of ideas per department. Names should not be used. Special variations include awarding the best idea each month or week. An award can be given to the department having 100 percent participation. For even more fun, the department with the worst participation can also receive a special reward. This program is successful only if it is run with a spirit of enthusiasm and fun—no fear or intimidation allowed.

IDEA BRAINSTORMING

This is usually done with a team or a group of people who normally work with each other. A facilitator helps the group brainstorm on a specific topic. For example, "How can we improve the assembly process?" or "How can we improve teamwork in our company?" Brainstorming is a good way to transition from individual suggestions to group ideas. There are specific **benefits** for using **idea brainstorming**:

→ Balances for the lack of individual experience.

→ Creates synergy that generates more ideas.

→ Uses a systematic approach.

→ Generates more ownership and team spirit.

Group sessions are always more fun, productive, and enthusiastic. It is best to use a facilitator and keep the group to no more than 8–10 people. The key in making idea brainstorming sessions work is to ask **open-ended questions** like the ones below:

→ If you were in charge, what would you do differently?

→ What ways can we improve the social environment in this organization?

→ What are the biggest time wasters?

→ What can we eliminate doing?

→ If you could change three things, what would they be?

→ If you had a magic wand, what would you change in the department?

IDEA OLYMPICS

Toyota was one the first companies to start Idea Olympics. The original form of Idea Olympics was an attempt to get people to think "out of the box." The goal was to get people away from the office environment to think creatively and innovatively about work. For example, a group of people or a team would have the meeting away from the office, maybe at a hotel or conference room. The group concentrates on new ways to reinvent the work process—a "no holds barred" think tank.

GOOD IDEA BOARDS

The Buckhead Ritz-Carlton Hotel has a unique way of capturing ideas and promoting continuous improvement from their front-line workers. Any worker who has a good idea writes it on an "easy wipe" board. Each department has this board on the wall. Instead of passing untested ideas up the chain of command, each employee who originates the idea has the responsibility for its achievement. They follow a three-step work process: "study it, pilot it and adopt it."

A quality coach assigned to each department assists employees with the process. Once the idea is piloted and found worthwhile, it is adopted. Each month the department decides who has the best idea. The idea is forwarded to the division and then on to the Quality Office for special recognition.

The department awards $10 to the employee with the best idea of the month. The best idea of the division gets $50 or brunch in the hotel's restaurant. At the hotel level, the best idea receives $100 or dinner for two. The winners receive letters of appreciation and an invitation to a quarterly reception courtesy of the Ritz-Carlton Hotel.

The good ideas don't have to be big. One innovative door attendant had the idea to pipe music into the first floor restroom. He took responsibility and went to see the engineering department. He talked to the director to see how hard it would be. There was a simple solution. Both he and the engineering director went to the restroom and found speakers and wire already in place. All they had to do was connect the wires and flip a switch, and the innovative idea came to life.

IDEA CAMPAIGNS

One of the most significant ways of improving employee involvement is the idea campaign. It represents an upgraded and streamlined version of the old employee suggestion program. Idea campaigns are one of the best ways of getting hundreds of ideas from your workforce in a very short time.

Ideas campaigns work hand in glove with all employee involvement programs. They can be used to kick start TQM, improve performance, identify problems that cause errors, generate revenue, and reduce expenses. For example, look at the following organizations who have done just that.

☺ Harley-Davidson saved $3,000,000 in one 30-day program.

☺ Holly Farms identified $1,000,000 in savings during a 4-week program.

☺ Eaton Corporation gained 944 ideas from a workforce of 113 people reaching 100 percent participation.

☺ Parker Hannifin Corporation submitted 499 ideas from 103 employees.

☺ National Semiconductor saved $3,600,000 using idea campaigns.

☺ The U.S. Park Service made over 12,000 suggestions with an approval rate of 75 percent.

Tremendous results, like the ones above, can be achieved by using idea programs. The Epic Healthcare Group of Irving, Texas, asked their employees to generate ideas that could be implemented and could generate at least $500 or more in profits during a 12-month period. The program was called Epic Excellence Ideas. Epic has over 9,028 employees in 39 hospitals nationwide. As many as 7,546 employees were put in seven-member teams to brainstorm ideas. Instead of monetary awards, teams were given credits for the suggestions.

To promote team spirit, each team member was given credits for the suggestion, even though he or she was not the originator of the suggestion. The credits were used to buy merchandise from a catalog of various awards. Epic's goal for the program was $9 million. To everyone's amazement, the program actually generated $21 million worth of ideas and improvements, 233 percent of the goal. One of the ideas generated was the establishment of an alcohol rehabilitation unit.

Eglin Air Force Base in Florida also ran an idea campaign. The campaign ran for two weeks. All employees and military personnel working on the base were asked to submit ideas that could reduce waste and inefficiency and increase productivity.

Eglin received a tremendous surprise when workers generated $400,000 worth of cost-saving ideas and ways to generate new forms of revenue. The director of the program said the greatest reward was not the money saved, but the excitement and enthusiasm he now sees in his people. He said, "...Once people have seen their ideas implemented, they are now stopping me in the hallway to give me new ideas."

There is a specific methodology behind running a successful idea campaign. There is a series of important steps that must be followed. Idea campaigns are not complicated, but if the steps are not completed, the entire campaign could backfire and could significantly injure morale and damage management credibility. When people trust you with their ideas, they are trusting you with a piece of their heart and minds. Forever cursed is the person who does not do anything with the ideas. Some of the **steps for a successful idea campaign** include:

→ **A marketing and communication plan**

→ **Teaser week**

→ **Rewards and recognition**

→ **Team leader training**

→ **Marketing materials, posters, banners, and idea forms**

→ **Leader involvement**

→ **Idea tracking system**

→ **Creating a sense of excitement**

Versions of the idea campaign can be provided by consultants, who provide assistance, all the materials, rewards, incentives, and instructional materials. There also are companies that can customize the idea campaign process to meet specific organizational needs.

Complimentary Aspects of
Employee Involvement Programs and Idea Campaigns

Involvement Programs	Idea Campaigns
Low acceptance rate	High acceptance rate
Bureaucratic	Easy
Boring	Fun
Long term	Short term
Low participation	High participation
Formal	Informal
Reward: Delayed	Reward: Immediate
Low intensity	High intensity
Broad focus	Specific focus
Paperwork and justifications	One small form

Slicing Through Administrative Trivia—STAT VA Idea Program

In the past, most VA hospitals resembled bureaucratic bastions surrounded by lines and lines of veterans waiting long hours for medical care. Today things are different.

Many VA hospitals have reinvented themselves into more caring and accessible health care facilities. The VA Medical Center in Portland is one of those that is changing. Their policy statement reflects this new change in philosophy. It includes these words:

It is the policy of this Medical Center to encourage creativity, problem-solving and innovation on the part of its employees at all levels.

One way the VA Medical Center in Portland brings this policy statement to life is through their innovative version of the venerable suggestion program. Their program is called STAT! (Slice Through Administrative Trivia) Idea Program. Creativity and innovation are encouraged throughout the medical center by this program. The STAT! Idea Program encourages all employees to look for innovations or changes in work procedures that might save time, effort, or costs in their work area or service. Ideas can relate to any area under the jurisdiction of the hospital.

Simplicity and fun are the hallmarks of this program. When employees come up with an idea, they first discuss it with the immediate supervisor. If the immediate supervisor agrees with the idea, it is then forwarded to the Service Chief, and the STAT! Idea form is sent to the STAT! Idea Committee.

It doesn't stop there. When a STAT! Idea is found to have wider application, the idea can be submitted to the Incentive Awards Suggestion Program for an even greater cash reward. The award process is what holds this program together. There are several levels of awards.

Any STAT! Idea implemented will generate an individual award for both the employee suggesting the idea and the immediate supervisor who approves the idea. Instead of killing the idea, this variation gives the supervisor an incentive to approve it. The first award is a choice of either a STAT! coffee mug or a STAT! writing pen. For the second and later ideas, both the employee and supervisor receive $10.00 for each idea implemented.

The STAT! Idea Committee reviews all ideas monthly and selects the best "Idea of the Month." The Best Idea of the Month receives both the $50.00 and the $10.00. Employees can submit as many ideas as they want. Monthly winners will be eligible for the "STAT! Idea of the Year" award. The award is $250 for both the employee and the supervisor.

The Committee selects the "Idea of the Year," deciding which department has the highest percentage of substantive implemented ideas per year. The winning department can receive upwards to $5,000. Many departments have split the money, using it to have a luncheon for the department, buy new furniture, a refrigerator for the break area, and new computers for the staff.

Getting MAD at Pacific Bell

Do you ever get MAD at the system? Frustrated with bureaucracy? Pacific Bell gets MAD all the time. MAD is a special work session that stands for, Make A Difference. The goal of these sessions is to:

"Do the things that Make A Difference"

"Change or Eliminate all the Rest"

MAD sessions are held off-site and designed to make tremendous changes in a short time. MAD sessions have several objectives including eliminating non-productive work, overcoming bureaucratic obstacles, increasing teamwork, sharing information, and acknowledging employee contributions.

Pacific Bell realized large organizations have a difficult time getting all the key players and decision makers together. A MAD session, or the abbreviated one-day Mini-MAD session, captures the workers and decision makers in one room. The process of combining both leaders and workers compresses decision cycles down from months to days, or even hours.

Kris Michaelis, Senior Organization Development Consultant, has seen this concept bloom and mature. She has experienced the effectiveness first hand. She says front-line workers and their supervisors enter the MAD session a little skeptically at first. They wonder if this is just another program, another waste of time. But when it is over, they leave with an entirely new and positive attitude.

Now these sessions have made major changes and improvements in Pacific Bell processes. However, Kris feels the greatest improvements come from workers who can see their ideas and input implemented immediately. They can see obstacles and barriers eliminated because the decision makers and the workers are all in the same room. No need for decision papers and a bureaucratic chain of command to go through. The secondary outcome is a workforce that gains more ownership. They have a clearer sense of why things happen. By reducing the "we/they" syndrome, people leave with a more trustful attitude of each other.

They make the MAD program more fun and zestful by using some special acronyms. They like to go "Fish Frying." The FISH acronym stands for: F—foolish

I—insipid

S—stupid

H—habit

During one session an individual changed the FISH acronym to a new one standing for Fine, Ideas, Should, Happen. Issues identified during the MAD session have their own fishy metaphors. MAD "Trouts" are smaller functions or pieces of work controlled by the work group. It may be one step in a lengthy process. Trouts can be eliminated without outside help. MAD "Marlins" are larger pieces of work, more complex in nature, crossing functional areas. They require outside support to catch and fry. Usually on the first day of the MAD, workers go fishing for trouts and gradually move up the food chain after the Marlins.

A typical three-day MAD session looks like this:

Day 1   9:00 A.M.–9:00 P.M.

Morning   Key business imperatives
               Paradigm shifts
               Customer panel
               Team norms

Afternoon   Functional teams work to eliminate/improve nonessential
               work

Evening   Team-building

Day 2   8:00 A.M.—9:00 P.M.

Morning   Presentation of FISH (Trout) "catches" and "fries" from
               functional teams
               Cross-functional team-building

Afternoon   Cross-functional teams work to eliminate nonessential work

Evening   Presentation of cross-functional FISH (Marlin) to senior
               leadership

Day 3   8:30 A.M.–3:00 P.M.

Morning   Senior management responds to cross-functional FISH
               (Marlin)
               Communication plan

Afternoon   Implementation commitments
               Transitioning back to work
               Session critique
               Closing session

Benefits from Using Idea Programs

Direct Benefits

Invigorates the Workplace
Makes work more productive
Creates a feeling of empowerment
Greater job satisfaction
Creates ownership and trust
Improves motivation and morale
Promotes cross functional teams
Identifies potential for cost reduction
Improves communication
Improves employee attitudes

Secondary Benefits

Can prevent layoffs if goal is cost cutting
Increases flow of information and communication
Shows a need for change and innovation
Used after mergers and reengineering efforts
Highlights National Quality Month
Help to implement Baldrige Criteria
Used as kick off for employee involvement programs
Focuses on internal customers
Creates a learning environment
Improves work processes

Management's Benefits

Increases profitability
Results pay for the cost of the program
Builds support for leadership team
Builds trust
Done quickly and efficiently
Minimal number of meetings

Employee Benefits

Opportunity to be heard by supervisors
Greater job satisfaction
Ability to contribute to the job
A way to make a major difference
Greater recognition and involvement
It is fun

STRONGER COMPANY   GROWING COMPANY

CHAPTER 12

TRANSFORMING WORKERS INTO WINNERS

"The aim of leadership should be to improve the performance of man and machine, to improve quality, to increase output, and simultaneously to bring pride of workmanship to people."
—Dr. Edwards Deming

Businesses face dynamic and ever increasing challenges. A global economy of discriminating consumers has placed demands on businesses never before seen. Managers face tasks of finding, keeping, and motivating workers. Environmental pressures, rising health care costs, and the sophisticated needs of the workforce have placed management in a complicated and tenuous situation. The answer lies with managing changes and creating an environment that motivates people toward exceptional performance.

People and their ideas make the winning difference in the innovative enterprise. Motivated people boost productivity challenging the competition, building worker pride, and increasing trust and loyalty. Recognition is the fuel that feeds the fire of motivation. Businesses who recognize that it is people who make the winning difference will be the most successful.

Bad Attitudes

In America today, workforce morale is a critical area of concern. Mergers, layoffs, and restructurings have had a negative impact on morale, motivation, and productivity. These workforce disruptions have promoted fear and lowered job satisfaction. Part of the problem was identified by Bradford Ray, a Roper researcher. He says, "Attitudes toward mergers have soured as people see those at the top getting generous pay, perks, and golden parachutes, while everybody else fears getting laid off."

Businesses have eliminated jobs but have not changed the workload. This has further soured attitudes and has eroded loyalty between the workers and management. Another striking problem is employee opinions of management. The HayGroup, a Philadelphia consulting group, surveyed more than a million employees. Their research showed that between 1987 and 1990, attitudes toward top management have dropped from "generally high" to "frankly awful."

Building motivation and morale requires a concentrated and continuous effort. It takes more than a few seminars, bonuses, and inspirational speeches by management. Motivation comes from giving workers pride in their work.

The Role of Motivation*

We must first ask the question, Why do we need motivated workers? The answer is simple—survival. The working world changes at a rapid pace. Technology reaches obsolescence at world record rates. A global marketplace puts tremendous demand on all businesses to stay competitive and create better and more advanced products and services. Successful businesses of the future will be only those that totally engage the creative abilities, talents, and potential of its workers. Motivated workers provide survival insurance.

---

*Information on motivation reprinted with permission of the publisher, from "Motivation" by Gregory P. Smith in *Human Resources Management and Development Handbook*, ed. R. Tracey. New York: AMACOM, 1994, pp. 253–51.

The most successful businesses are those that provide motivating environments. Seeking ways to motivate and build worker morale pays dividends to any business or organization. Motivated employees create the most productive workplaces. The motivated worker is more committed to the job. In a demotivating environment, workers vote with their feet. They can become stagnant and slow down progress. Unmotivating workplaces have higher turnover, and individual employees may look for more desirable employment elsewhere.

The Challenge

Walk into a health club during lunch, and you will see men and women exercising. They are lifting weights, riding cycles, doing aerobics, and perspiring. Why do people enjoy doing something that appears, to an outsider, to be a painful process? No one ordered them to go out on the exercise floor and perspire. They are all volunteers. Something motivated them. Similarly, go into an office on Friday and notice the attitude. Why is it that people seem more enthusiastic on Fridays than on Mondays? What is the common motivating factor in an office on a Friday and in a health club?

Motivation is a process or a set of forces that causes a person to behave in a certain manner. The resulting behavior can be either positive (movement toward a certain goal) or negative (away from a goal). These sets of forces or motives can be either social, spiritual, financial, or psychological. The forces can be a set of basic needs, wishes, desires, and dreams. These forces are called either motivators or demotivators. Motivators move us toward a particular goal while demotivators move us away from a goal.

The day-to-day challenge managers' face is how to motivate people to be productive workers. If they can be motivated on an exercise floor, why are they unmotivated at work? The main question is, "Why do they do what they do?"

Fran Tarkenton says, to find what motivates people, "...You have to find what turns people on." How do you provide an environment that transforms workers from unmotivated employees into motivated winners? How do you change ordinary people into extraordinary employees? The secret of success is understanding what motivates people and getting them to go from having to do something to choosing to do something.

Money as a Motivator

Many discussions have centered on the role of money and financial incentives as a motivating force. It can be concluded that its impact remains controversial but plays an important role. The impact of money for some people is an important motivator, and for others, it isn't. More importantly, the absence of it serves as a strong demotivator. Despite the controversy surrounding financial incentives, the motivating effect of money can be maximized in light of the following points.

Money is important in maintaining an acceptable standard of living. Employees expect enough money to meet their needs and hopefully have enough left over for the future. Younger workers just starting out in the business world may be more concerned about money than more experienced workers. It is important to note that money becomes a demotivator when compensation does not meet basic needs. When people are financially comfortable, the motivating impact of money is minimized.

The work environment plays a significant role concerning money as a motivating factor. During a period of high unemployment, the amount of money is not as important as having job security. Workers are likely to feel thankful for having a job rather than how much they are being paid. Businesses need to concentrate on factors that motivate workers other than just financial incentives. Intangible factors are usually more motivational than financial incentives. To some people, the friendliness of the work environment is more important than the amount of money they make. During positive economic times, money can reduce turnover and insure the best people stay with a particular employer. In a competitive environment, money becomes much more important to people. In summary, financial incentives are more motivational during a secure economy than when joblessness is high.

Money and motivation are critically related in relation to perceived and actual financial differences between individual co-workers and managers. Here again, money serves more as a demotivator than a motivator. Workers must feel a sense of equity. In many cases, managers' salaries are disproportionately higher than that of ordinary workers. A cartoon I discovered recently highlighted this situation.

The cartoon illustrated a discussion between a manager and his employee. They were discussing their salaries. The manager told his worker that he didn't like his $300,000 salary any more than the employee liked his $30,000 salary, "but he didn't whine about it."

A final factor is the pay-for-performance issue. Business performance is significantly improved when pay and bonuses are linked to individual performance. In many situations, however, special pay and allowances only go to managers and not to individual workers. This gives workers a bad feeling that management is more important than they are. Linking pay to performance for everyone, not just managers, will increase individual motivation, ownership, and responsibility.

Management's Responsibility

Before we can understand or build employee motivation and morale, we must first understand management's responsibility. In the military, the commander's responsibilities are clearly delegated. Basically put, Army commanders are responsible for everything his/her unit does or fails to do. In the civilian world, the manager or leader has similar responsibilities. The success or failure of the business greatly depends on its leadership and the decisions the leaders make.

The Role of the Leader

Dr. Edwards Deming says, "The aim of leadership should be to improve the performance of man and machine, to improve quality, to increase output, and simultaneously to bring pride of workmanship to people." He continues by adding, "The aim of leadership

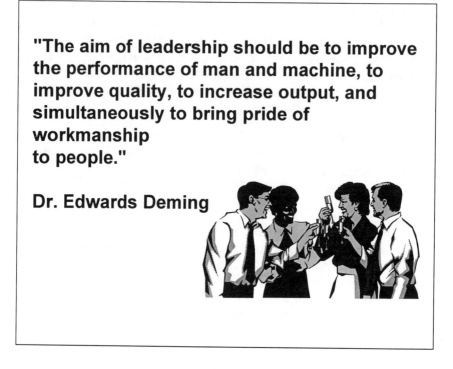

"The aim of leadership should be to improve the performance of man and machine, to improve quality, to increase output, and simultaneously to bring pride of workmanship to people."

Dr. Edwards Deming

is not merely to find and record failures of men, but to remove the causes of failure: to help people to do a better job with less effort." One of the major responsibilities of a leader is to create a positive working environment, provide motivating leadership, and train the workers to do the job. However, critics are quick to show that many businesses have not provided the kind of leadership that motivates employees for superior performance.

A Bigger View of Work

A job is more significant than most people realize. Most people of the world devote more time and energy at work than they do at home. Jobs provide more than income to employees or a product or service for the employer. A job provides self-esteem, status, social contact, self-worth, and other intangible benefits to people. Understanding this gives us an indication of how motivation may rest with understanding people's needs. Management has great responsibility in creating motivating workplaces. Management can create two types of workplaces—a motivating or a demotivating workplace.

The Motivation Process

Creating a motivating workplace follows a specific process. Motivation, like other things in life, does not occur naturally. A motivation process involves a series of steps that helps create a motivated workplace. These steps can be obvious, like building an on-site day care facility, or subtle, such as a feeling of trust between management and employees. The success or failure of the process depends on leadership.

Leadership is responsible for creating a motivational environment. Managers cannot sit passively behind a desk and create motivated people. They must be actively involved and foster a work environment that motivates people. Managers must discover ways and means that motivate people to exceptional performance. Applying motivational theories often fails because these approaches focus only on making workers change without requiring management to change. The first step in the process is to create a motivating environment.

Creating such an environment is probably the most important step in the motivation process. An *environment* is a set of dynamic forces that either positively or negatively influences the behavior and attitudes of workers.

In the world today, people are concerned about a variety of environments. Of great concern to people is the natural environment. After many decades of abuse, we have realized how fragile the natural environment is. Much money and many resources are spent controlling pollution and protecting endangered species.

The business environment has a more immediate and more far-reaching impact than the natural environment. Within the business environment, there are qualities that make the environment motivational or demotivational. The business environment is the building block for a motivated organization. Motivated people build a motivational organization.

The Importance of Trust

Trust between managers and workers is paramount for motivation. Employees want to trust their managers. Natural obstacles to trust and candor are fear, politics, pride, perceptions, and bureaucratic rules and regulations. Managers display trust in many verbal and nonverbal ways. Management's consistency in action is a sign of trust. Does management do what it says? A company that promises permanent employment and then later lays off workers damages trust. A company that promises newly hired employees career advancement but provides no training violates its trust. Countless unspoken and spoken acts eat away at the trust reservoir gradually destroying morale and motivation. Trust is easy to destroy and takes a long time to build.

How to Motivate People—The Pride System

A major aim of leadership is to improve the performance of workers and help them take pride in the quality of their work. Leaders can improve motivation within their organizations by following the PRIDE system. The PRIDE System is a five-step process that helps build motivation.

P   Provide for a positive working environment.

R   Recognize everyone's efforts.

I   Involve everyone.

D   Develop skills and potential.

E   Evaluate and measure continuously.

STEP 1   PROVIDE FOR PEOPLE'S NEEDS

Walt Disney World Company in Orlando, Florida, provides excellent service to their employees or "cast members." Employee assistance centers are spread strategically across the theme park. Some of the services provided include discount programs, KinderCare information, money orders, postage stamps, check cashing, and bus passes, to name a few. The Walt Disney Company realizes taking care of employee needs keeps them motivated and on the job.

To motivate people, you must first provide for their needs. This is the most important factor in the motivation process. The workforce of this decade is different from that of any previous decade. Now, more than ever, workers are influencing the character of work. An economy of fax machines, computers, electronic mail, and tele-conferencing has created a workforce unlike any other. To motivate people we must understand all the dynamic forces, needs, and challenges that impact the workforce today.

A transformation has taken place during the past 20 years. We have changed from an industrial age of factories and manufacturing plants to an age of information and service. A more educated workforce has increased job expectations. Workers want to have more control and want to participate more within their jobs. In many cases, they are more qualified than some of their supervisors. A transformation has taken place changing most workers from blue collar jobs to a nation of white collar workers. Within the world of white-collar workers, a new type of worker has arrived— the Gold-Collar worker. These people are highly skilled, creative, and independent. They consistently meet and exceed the goals. This is why they are called Gold-Collar workers. Motivating the Gold-Collar workers requires special abilities. They work best when they are given independence, kept informed, given additional responsibilities when possible, and given challenging assignments. Occasionally, they are stubborn and demanding. They will rebel against perceived trivial or meaningless tasks. Management must realize, if they are dissatisfied, these people can easily find employment elsewhere. Management expert Robert E. Kelly describes them as "giving their managers gray hair while constantly escalating the organization's profits."

People today have more sophisticated needs. They attend to instant gratification and want their needs satisfied more quickly. Their frustration increases and motivation suffers when they feel management is not meeting their needs. Managers can meet needs faster by using technology and communication more frequently.

Electronic mail, fax machines, and frequent staff meetings can help spread information and reduce time lag.

Federal Express has accurately diagnosed the key to building morale and motivation. Their philosophy reflects how they feel about their employees. They believe that their "PEOPLE" (employees) come first. They, in turn, deliver excellent SERVICE to their customers, and PROFIT will follow. It is a philosophy based on employee satisfaction first. Employee satisfaction leads to customer satisfaction.

The home and the problems surrounding home-life have a tremendous impact on job productivity. Today's fast-paced, complex society has replaced social support groups found in the early 1900s. The church, the neighborhood, and the family were the bedrocks of American society. Now, workers' only source of social interaction may be the job. There are more single parents working on the job than ever before. The impact of aging parents, maternity and paternity needs, and the impact of health needs will continue to be challenges for supervisors. Recent laws have been passed that have given additional benefits to workers with families. Years ago, the military told soldiers to leave their personal problems at home, the mission always came first. Today, wise leaders realize that the home and the family significantly impact on motivation and job performance.

STEP 2   RECOGNIZE EVERYONE'S EFFORTS

The second step is personal recognition of everyone's efforts. Mark Twain once said, "I can live for two months on a good compliment." More recently, George Blomgren, President of Organizational Psychologists, said, "Recognition lets people see themselves in a winning identity role. There's a universal need for recognition and most people are starved for it."

A pat on the back, a personal note from the supervisor or a small celebration can do wonders for building morale. Personal recognition plays a vital role when realizing that recognition reinforces and encourages the same behavior. If positive behavior is reinforced, it will repeat itself. Unfortunately, these tools are often overlooked.

A worker in the tax office of a large hotel chain has worked hard for the last two months. She was able to save the company $15,000 by taking advantage of a little known tax law. She was proud of her accomplishment, and she shared her success with her family at the dinner table. The next day, she carefully prepared a memo telling her supervisor how she implemented this new procedure and how she saved the money. She never heard anything back from the supervisor.

The most productive businesses are those where every worker is highly involved in the business enterprise. In reality, most businesses only encourage a few outstanding performers. The vast majority of workers usually go unnoticed. These above-average workers are usually self-starters who for one reason or another have captured management's eye. The top performers usually get all the recognition while the majority feels left out and uncared for. **The failure to recognize the accomplishments of the majority of the workers may be one of the greatest reasons why managers fail to create a motivating work environment.**

There are two primary reasons for management's failure to recognize workers' accomplishments. First, many supervisors are too detached from the day-to-day trials and tribulations of the "ordinary" worker. It's easier to reward the top performers because they are clearly seen. Recognition will encourage the ordinary worker to do better.

The second reason managers fail to motivate people is that they practice the 80/20 rule. Performance of most people is usually good 80 percent of the time and could be better 20 percent of the time. However, managers concentrate on the 20 percent. They tend to concentrate and blame workers for failures instead of concentrating on the 80 percent of the good.

When the space shuttle Challenger exploded, a gigantic witch hunt began to find the person or company responsible for the disaster. People were fired, and resignations were accepted. Careers of thousands of hard working people and innocent lives were damaged or ruined. Morale and job dedication plummeted. Yes, the reason for the explosion needed to be discovered and corrected, but more time and energy often goes into blaming people than preventing the problems in the first place. Managers need to either fix the problem or prevent it, instead of fixing the blame.

The following items summarize the impact recognition has on the workforce:

→ Behavior that is recognized reinforces that same behavior. If management wants something to continue, they must recognize those people doing it.

→ Effective recognition does not have to be monetary. Effective recognition must be timely and sincere. Little things can mean a lot to workers. Managers who go out of their way to discover good behavior will be rewarded with more motivated workers.

→ In order to effect a change in behavior, a specific behavior must be extensively rewarded and recognized. If an organization wants to transform from a hierarchal type of organization to a horizontally oriented or team-oriented environment, team-oriented behaviors must be rewarded and recognized. Recognition of traditional behavior will only continue to reinforce traditional behavior.

→ Negative consequences will demotivate that behavior. If management wants to extinguish a certain behavior, they must use the appropriate consequences to stop it.

→ Positive reinforcement must be continuous in order to maintain positive behavior. A new program often starts with great fanfare, only to be replaced by another program later on.

STEP 3   INVOLVE EVERYONE

Involving all workers at all levels of the business has merit, not only in building morale and motivation, but it has a major impact on improving profit and productivity. Getting workers involved requires following certain steps. First, increase communication within the entire workforce. Second, develop teams. Third, empower all workers to make decisions that will positively impact their job.

Robert Half, a human resources consultant, conducted a survey in 1988. He concluded that workers were wasting 4 1/2 hours a week. This cost employers $200 billion a year. Experts feel management is part of the blame. The reasons workers goof-off are many but can generally be put into one of the following categories:

→ Employers setting bad examples.

→ Unchallenging work.

→ Employers not involved.

→ Workers not empowered.

→ Work not efficiently organized.

→ No established goals.

Increase Communication. The goal of communication is to narrow the gap between top management and the lowest level worker. Management must know what workers are thinking. Attempts to maximize communication includes all forms of verbal and written communication. The military practices something called "gripe sessions." Senior leaders meet with lower-ranking troops. In this environment, troops will openly communicate gripes and perceptions. The information allows military leaders to know exactly what is going on. Sometimes this is a painful experience for the leaders. It must be conducted frequently and in a non-defensive manner. Even though management may be able to do nothing about the problems, the troops feel someone at the top is listening to them.

According to a 1991 issue of *Fortune* magazine, the most useful form of communication that improves productivity is regular meetings with employees. Meetings conducted in a brown-bag-lunch atmosphere is another way to close the gap. Frequent meetings in a casual atmosphere aid in building communication in many businesses. Employees are able to state gripes and ask questions.

Satisfaction surveys are another way of communicating between the lower and higher level employees. In times of stress, communication is more important. W. Thomas Stephens, Chairman of the Manville Corporation, says, "We learned that, in times of stress, communication has to increase exponentially, or you won't survive."

Develop Teamwork and Self-Directed Teams. Businesses are finding teamwork is improving morale and productivity. A team usually consists of small clusters of 7–15 people each. Team members include representatives from various departments. They either work together in a permanent or a temporary capacity. Members of the teams work together toward a particular goal or process. Teamwork allows the return of control back to the workers. The result is less need for excessive numbers of middle managers and supervisors.

Teams have many benefits not available in traditional work environments. Teamwork makes workers more productive by overcoming the normal frictions between workers and interdepartmental strife. Teamwork engages workers' minds as well as their bodies. Significant improvements have occurred in manufacturing plants where teams control the entire assembly process. Teams decide when parts are assembled and who assembles them. They schedule shifts and in some cases, they decide who is hired and fired. Advocates of teamwork feel it gives workers feelings of dignity and self-worth. Teamwork seems to be superior to Quality Circles because employees have the authority to carry out all team-made decisions.

Empower All Employees. William J. O'Brian, CEO of Hanover Insurance Company, says, "The fundamental movement in business in the next 25 years will be in dispersing of power, to give meaning and fulfillment to employees in a way that avoids chaos and disorder."

Managers need to empower employees and give them more control over their jobs. By increasing the level of responsibility, workers will take more pride in their jobs. Expanded responsibilities mean less time spent doing menial tasks. Empowered workers need less supervision and fewer supervisors. Aetna Life & Casualty increased the ratio between workers and middle management from 1/7 up to 1/30 and at the same time improved customer service.

Traditional management theory dictates a small span of control. Management schools have recommended one supervisor for every seven workers. Using a combination of empowerment and teamwork, one supervisor or team leader is sufficient for 20-30 workers. "Downsizing," "flattening the pyramid," and "corporate streamlining," refer to the process of bringing the executive leadership closer to the front-line, lower-level worker.

STEP 4   DEVELOP PEOPLE'S SKILLS AND POTENTIAL

Businesses gain many benefits from highly trained and developed employees. The German poet, Goethe, said, "Treat people as though they were what they ought to be and you will help them become what they are capable of being." Many American businesses are discovering what Japanese businesses found out a long time ago—people are the secret to success in a global marketplace. One benefit of employee development is that employees are more capable and willing to assume more control over their jobs. They need less supervision, which frees management for other tasks. Employees gain a more thorough understanding of management's problems, goals, and challenges. Employees who have a better understanding of how the business works are less likely to complain or to be dissatisfied and more likely to be motivated. All this leads to better manager-employee relationships.

United States Automobile Association (USAA) spends nearly twice the industry average on training, 2.7 percent of it's annual budget. In 1991 they gave $1.4 million in college tuition to their employees. Employees feel USAA is a great place to work because of its emphasis on training. Training and education motivates people to be more productive and innovative. Tom Peters, co-author of *Passion For Excellence,* says during tough economic times, businesses should increase training. The more versatile and more highly trained workers are, the more productive they become. That is particularly true for lower-level workers. Studies show that Japanese auto workers receive three times the amount of training each year than their U.S. counterparts. Japanese imports have been rated the most reliable automobiles for many years running. The little money that is spent on training in the United States usually goes to salespeople, executives, and technical personnel.

At Federal Express, all employees who have direct customer contact are given six weeks of training before they ever answer the first phone call. Learning never stops and testing continues throughout their employment tenure. Every six months customer service people are tested using an on-line computer system. Pass/fail results are sent to each employee within 24 hours. They receive a personalized "prescription" on areas that need improvement, along with a list of resources and lessons that will help. Their intensive training and development program results in better morale and motivation.

STEP 5   EVALUATE CONTINUOUSLY

Evaluate continuously is the final step of the PRIDE system. Evaluation is a never-ending cycle. Continuous evaluation must lead to continuous improvement. Efforts toward continuous improvement should concentrate on improving the quality of work life for the individual employee. Once the employee's quality of life is improved, the quality of the business will improve accordingly. The entire evaluation cycle contributes to the improvement of the nation as a whole.

Dr. Yoshi Tsurumi provides another approach. He says,

Part of America's industrial problems is the aim of its corporate managers. Most American executives think they are in business to make money, rather than products and service...The Japanese corporate credo, on the other hand, is that a company should become the world's most efficient provider of whatever product and service it offers. Once it becomes the world leader and continues to offer good products, profits follow.

Continuous evaluation and never-ending improvement are key components in keeping a competitive edge. Old sayings like, "good enough for government work" and "if it ain't broken, don't fix it" are falling victim to more proactive strategies. One of my favorite books is, *If It Ain't Broke, Break It*, by Robert J. Kriegel. This book stretches the paradigm by showing us the importance of continuously improving everything the business does and never being satisfied with the status quo. Those managers sitting in the driver's seat waiting for the squeaky wheel to squeak may already be in big trouble.

Evaluation and continuous improvement are nonstop activities following a specific cycle of steps. The primary purpose of evaluation is to measure progress and decide what needs improving. Evaluation includes, but is not limited to, the measurement of customer satisfaction, measurement of waste and rework, purchase order cycle time, morale, and motivation of the workforce. Areas identified needing improvement are included in an improvement plan. Managers rank which business areas are the most important deserving attention. Improvement teams are formed and assigned areas of responsibility and deadlines. Key managers monitor progress and keep the teams on course. The evaluation process leads to continuous improvement.

Japanese businesses designed the Check-Act-Plan-Do process for evaluating and measuring continuous improvement. Americans have a similar version called the PDCA (Plan-Do-Check-Act) cycle. For simplicity, I use the Japanese version, but still call it the PDCA cycle. The cycle is explained below:

PDCA CYCLE

1. **CHECK—Evaluate and analyze a situation. For example, you discover worker productivity is dropping in one of your departments. Your first step is to gather objective information and relevant data. During this process you discover higher-than-normal personnel turnover and increased sick-leave use.**

2. **ACT—You make a decision to call some of the employees working in the department. You ask them for their opinions and the reasons why certain things are happening. You talk with other managers and associates, trying to obtain as much information as possible.**

3. **PLAN—Once you fully understand the problem, you map out a strategy on how to solve it. You outline the necessary steps in chronological order. You consider the alternatives and possible outcomes of each action you take.**

4. **DO—Having completed the planning process, you outline the decision and implement changes accordingly. Once changes are carried out, follow up, measure progress, and improve continuously.**

The PDCA cycle begins each time a problem/situation is encountered or until every key business area meets the highest level of quality possible.

As was mentioned in the discussion of the PRIDE system, Federal Express has a beneficial way of measuring morale and employee satisfaction. They have a "people-first" philosophy. They measure how employees feel with an annual Survey Feedback Action (SFA). The survey gives employees a chance to express their feelings about their company, their supervisors, the service, benefits, and pay. Every year, it is filled out anonymously by each work group. Each answer on the survey has one of three responses: "favorable," "sometimes favorable," or "unfavorable." The overall results are given to each manager. He/she must meet with their group and discuss the results and come up with a plan of action to solve any problems. The scores for the entire management are tallied together into one score. If the company-wide leadership score is lower than the previous year's score, no one in management receives a yearly bonus. Everyone at Federal Express has pay-for-performance, including the founder and CEO, Fred Smith.

Summary

Today's business leaders are concerned about how to make businesses competitive and productive, and at the same time provide a quality product or service. The search for the competitive advantage has been aggressively debated far and wide. Advanced technology can provide a competitive edge, but true productivity will only be advanced by people. People who are motivated work together toward the particular goal or goals of the enterprise. The catalyst that provides the motivation is quality leadership.

Leadership is responsible for the success or failure of the business. John D. Rockefeller said, "The primary goal of good management is to show average people how to do the work of superior people." Leadership is responsible for creating a motivating environment. A motivating environment is one that instills a sense of pride in the workers. Leaders must take time to know the people they lead. They must provide for their needs, recognize their efforts, involve them in all aspects of the business, develop them, and evaluate continuously. These steps, once completed, will help win the hearts and minds of the worker. A motivated worker will contribute vitality and energy and will make the business become productive and competitive while providing a valuable service or product.

ORGANIZATIONAL ASSESSMENT

This organizational assessment will help you determine the level of morale and motivation in your organization. The answers to these questions will give you an accurate indication of what particular areas may need improving.

1. Workplace Environment

   a. Are there more rules in the organization that tell people what they can't do versus what they can do?

   b. Are there rules, policies, procedures that humiliate or provide preferential treatment to a certain group of employees?

   c. Are workers doing meaningful work or busy work? Are they creating or providing a quality service or manufacturing a quality product? Are they proud of what they do?

   d. Does the work environment support and accommodate change and flexibility?

e. Is there openness between management and workers that promotes trust and candor?

f. Are the promises made to workers kept? Are the promises made in the employee handbook maintained?

2. Rewards and Recognition

a. Does the organization use rewards and recognition liberally?

b. Is there a formal review process on use of rewards and recognition? Are there people not getting the recognition that they deserve?

c. Are there frequent, small, celebrations of victories and accomplishments?

3. Leadership

a. Are senior executives personally involved and visible throughout the organization?

b. Is middle management visible and actively involved with workers at all levels?

c. Does management really know what is going on within the organization?

d. Does the leadership instill appropriate values and standards in the workers?

e. Does the vision of the organization inspire and motivate people to a higher goal?

f. Does management listen frequently to all workers of the organization?

g. Have the strengths and weaknesses of the employees been accurately assessed so that tasks capitalize on their strengths?

4. People

a. Are workers provided with training and career development programs?

b. Does the organization involve families with business functions?

c. Is there some form of child care assistance provided for the employees?

d. Are employees involved in some form of teamwork? Are they empowered to make decisions?

e. Are all employees involved in a profit-sharing program?

f. Does the company measure employee turn-over? Is it getting better or worse?

g. Have employees been allowed to set goals and help decide how to achieve them?

h. Are employees who leave the organization interviewed before they depart?

i. Is there some form of flex-time available to workers?

APPENDIX A

Business Term Glossary

Benchmarking—a continuous, systematic process for evaluating the products, services and work processes of organizations recognized as representing best practices for organizational improvement.

Continuous Quality Improvement (CQI)—the process of organizational incremental improvement. It is constant and infinite. This word is used in many healthcare organizations.

Customers—people, organizations or groups receiving the products and/or services of people within. A customer can be external or internal. An example of an internal customer would be anyone within your organization that you provide information or service to. An external customer is someone not directly in your organization but who depends on you as a supplier of some process, product, or service.

Customer-Oriented Culture—a working environment that focuses on the quality of its work based on feedback from customers.

Customer-Focused Policy—outlines the constraints and guidelines to help create the development of a customer-oriented culture.

Delayering—the process of removing layers of supervisors and organizational structure. The goal is to bring top management, or the decision makers, closer to the front-line worker.

Downsizing/Rightsizing—a surgical approach to eliminating people from businesses. This is probably the most commonly used approach and sometimes least effective way to improve profitability.

Empowerment—an understood authority for employees to act (e.g., make changes), take responsibility, and accept accountability.

Kaizen—a Japanese-style productivity system focusing on capturing ideas from the workforce. It is more advanced than the American suggestion program, capturing 48 million ideas from Japanese employees in 1986. Toyota gained 2.65 million suggestions from its employees.

Key Business Drivers—areas of performance that are the most critical to the organization's success. They can include customer-driven quality and operational requirements such as productivity, cycle time, deployment of new technology, strategic alliances, supplier development, and R&D. It is also important to measure customer satisfaction, customer retention and market share.

Leader—a person who practices the art of leadership and inspires you to take a journey to a destination you wouldn't go by yourself.

Malcolm Baldrige National Quality Award—an award sponsored by the federal government. It exists within the private sector and provides an assessment tool to help organizations seek the highest levels of overall quality performance and competitiveness.

Management By Walking Around (MBWA)—getting out of the office and having contact with the workforce. Gives executives and employees an opportunity to exchange information informally. Hewlett-Packard, for instance, has weekly get-togethers where information flows freely and executives can stay in touch. They get a "feel" for the atmosphere within the company and gain quick and easy access to information.

Managers—people who influence the use and consumption of resources.

Organizational Support Services—internal service areas such as information systems, public affairs, procurement, facilities management, administrative services, etc.

Ownership—a sense of responsibility and involvement in a process, product, service, or policy.

Quality and Customer Focus—a strategic vision that defines goals to drive the organization, which holds quality and customers as the most valued assets.

Quality Performance Management System—a defined system that involves the vision, quality values and customer focus, which holds quality as the main focus to measure performance.

Quality and Operational Performance Improvement Goals—quality-related goals that pertain to improving the day-to-day functions of individuals/teams within the organization.

Quality Values—beliefs established and supported by the organization's culture that drives the standards for all products and services.

Reengineering—made popular by Dr. Michael Hammer, author of *Reengineering the Corporation.* Hammer says, "Reengineering is the fundamental rethinking and radical redesign of business processes to achieve dramatic improvements in critical, contemporary measures of performance, such as cost, quality, service, and speed." This means streamlining everything in the cycle of completing the process of work. Find the quickest, most direct route to accomplish the job. If it doesn't add value, get rid of it.

Reframing—a word coined by Gemini Consulting, which denotes the constant vigilance about whether the vision, strategies, and objectives of a company need to be changed or amended.

Retrenchment—designates the reduction in scope of diversification. In the 80s and early 90s, many companies diversified into industries they knew little or nothing about. They expended a lot of energy and capital, only to find that profitability did not improve, and the core business suffered. So, retrenchment is the re-concentration on the core business accompanied by the divestment of unrelated businesses that do not have a strategic fit.

Senior Leaders/Executives—the organization's highest ranking officials and those reporting directly to that official.

Strategy and Planning—refer to the future-oriented basis for major business decisions, resource allocations, and company-wide management.

Supervisors—anyone who supervises another person or groups of personnel.

Support Services—services that support the organization's product and/or service delivery but are not usually designed in detail with the products and services themselves.

Suppliers—people or organizations that provide materials, information, products and/or services to your organization.

Team—any group of two or more people working together toward a common goal.

Total Quality Management (TQM)—a management system or culture for achieving exceptional customer satisfaction by involving everyone in the business. TQM taps the potential, abilities, skills, and knowledge laying dormant in the American worker. TQM combines the world's best management tools and techniques.

Value-Added Work—steps that either add value or detract from the value of the work, called non-value added. For example, you apply for a house mortgage at your local bank. The application is completed and routed to various checkers, auditors, and approvers within the bank bureaucracy, until finally someone stamps it, "Approved." Everyone who touches this application should be adding value, adding something positive to the process.

Vision—a challenging image that coveys a future image to everyone of what the organization stands for, where it is heading and how it will reach it's destination. It has the potential to motivate and inspire and to lead people to a particular destination.

APPENDIX B

Malcolm Baldrige National Quality Award Criteria

1.0   LEADERSHIP

1.1   Senior Executive Leadership

Describe senior executives' leadership and personal involvement in setting directions and in developing and maintaining a leadership system for performance excellence.

1.2   Leadership and Organization

Describe how the organization's customer focus and performance expectations are integrated into the organization's leadership system and operating structure.

> 1.2a System, Organization, Management, and Process Arrangement Facilitate Performance and Customer Satisfaction
>
> The organization's leadership system, management, and work units focus on customer objectives in the following ways. Customer objectives include customer feedback, customer participation, customer training, and customer cross-training with the agency's own staff. High performance objectives include a procedure process map of the organization's leadership system and linkages with listed objectives. Objectives may also include supervisor to employee ratio, employee empowerment, and

performance improvement bodies such as the ESC, Quality Management Board (QMB), PATs, and Cross-Functional Teams.

1.2b Deployment of Values, Expectations and Direction

The organization effectively communicates and reinforces its values, expectations, and directions throughout the work force in the following ways. Include a variety of media, communications, and training used to deliver the organization's values and expectations. List two-way communications that take place. One example is putting a section in the newspaper for people recognition, publishing new ideas, and reinforcing values, expectations and directions.

1.2c Organizational Performance Review

Organization and work unit performance is reviewed and used to improve performance in a number of ways. Describe the types, frequency, and content of reviews and who conducts them. Some reviews are added work and detract from value. They are a measure of waste and are defined as waste. What is being done to correct the process to reduce review time? Reviews should utilize information from business and customer-related results, as well as Performance Review and Report results used by leadership to update the Strategic Planning Process. Descriptions should address key measures and/or indicators used to track performance, including performance related to the organization's public responsibilities. One example of sharing data and information is through your Local Area Network (LAN). The organization should also review critical processes. A PAT could be used to develop ways and methods to improve areas which are out of tolerance.

1.3   Public Responsibility and Corporate Citizenship

Describe how the organization includes its responsibilities to the public in its performance improvement practices. Describe also how the organization leads and contributes as a corporate citizen in its key communities.

2.0   INFORMATION AND ANALYSIS

2.1   Management of Information and Data

Describe the organization's selection and management of information/data used for planning, management, and evaluation of overall performance.

2.2   Competitive Comparisons and Benchmarking

Describe the organization's processes and uses of comparative information and data to support improvement of overall performance.

2.3   Analysis and Use of Organization-Level Data

Information and data from all parts of the organization are integrated and analyzed to support reviews, business decisions, and planning. Describe how analysis is used to gain understanding in the areas of customers and markets, operational performance and organization capabilities and competitive understanding.

3.0   STRATEGIC PLANNING

3.1   Strategy Development

Describe the organization's strategic planning process for overall performance and competitive leadership for the short term and the long term. Describe also how this process leads to the development of key business drivers to serve as the basis for deploying plan requirements throughout the organization.

3.2   Strategy Deployment

Summarize the organization's key business drivers and how they are deployed. Show how the organization's performance projects into the future relative to competitors and key benchmarks. The focus here is on the translation of the organization's strategic plans, resulting from the process described in Item 3.1, to requirements for work units, suppliers and partners. This item aligns short- and long-term operations with strategic directions. Include a clearly defined deployment plan complete with timelines.

4.0   HUMAN RESOURCE DEVELOPMENT AND MANAGEMENT

4.1   Human Resource Planning and Evaluation

Describe how the organization's human resource planning and evaluation are aligned with its strategic and business plans and address the development and well-being of the entire work force. This item examines how well the work force is empowered to develop its full potential, and to see how the work force is aligned with the organization's performance objectives. It examines how the organization builds and maintains an environment that is conducive to performance excellence, and how this environment promotes personal and organizational growth.

4.2   High Performance Work Systems

Describe how the organization's work and job design and compensation and recognition approaches enable and encourage all members to contribute effectively to achieving high performance objectives.

4.3   Organization Member Education, Training, and Development

Describe how the organization's education and training address work unit plans, including building on existing capabilities and contributing to member motivation, progression, and development.

4.4   Organization Member Well-Being and Satisfaction

Describe how the organization maintains a work environment and climate conducive to the well-being and development of all organization members.

5.0   PROCESS MANAGEMENT

5.1   Design and Introduction of Products and Services

Describe how new and/or modified products and services are designed and introduced and how key production/delivery processes are designed to meet both key product and service quality requirements.

5.2   Process Management: Product and Service Production and Delivery

Describe how the organization's key product and service production/ delivery processes are managed to ensure that design requirements are met and that both quality and operational performance are continuously improved.

5.3   Process Management: Support Services

Describe how the organization's key support service processes are designed and managed so that current requirements are met and that operational performance is continuously improved. Support services support the organization's product and/or service delivery but are not usually designed in detail with the products and services themselves because their requirements do not usually depend a great deal upon product and service characteristics.

5.4   Management of Supplier Performance

Describe how the organization assures that materials, components, and services furnished by other businesses meet the organization's requirements. Describe also the organization's actions and plans to improve supplier relationships and performance.

6.0   BUSINESS RESULTS

6.1   Product and Service Quality Results

Summarize results of improvement efforts using key measures and/or indicators of product and service quality.

6.2   Organizational Operational and Financial Results

Summarize results of improvement efforts using key measures and/or indicators of the organization's operational and financial performance. This item should address the areas of productivity, cycle time and responsiveness, financial indicators, human resource indicators, public responsibilities, and organization-specific indicators.

6.3   Supplier Performance Results

Summarize results of supplier performance improvement efforts using key measures and/or indicators of such performance.

Results reported in this item derive from activities described in Item 5.4. Results should be broken out by key supplies and/or key suppliers. Examples include how well suppliers perform considering the quality, delivery and price of products and services as well as expected performance levels, and how well supplier relationships are developed.

7.0   CUSTOMER FOCUS AND SATISFACTION

7.1   Customer and Market Knowledge

Describe how the organization determines near-term and longer-term requirements and expectations of customers and businesses, and develops listening and learning strategies to understand and anticipate needs.

7.2   Customer Relationship Management

Describe how the organization provides effective management of its responses and follow-ups with customers to preserve and build relationships and to increase knowledge about specific customers and about general customer expectations.

Customer relationship management refers to a process, not to an organizational unit, although some organizations may have units which address all or most of the requirements included in this item.

7.3   Customer Satisfaction Determination

Describe how the organization determines customer satisfaction, customer purchase intentions, and customer satisfaction relative to competitors, and how these determination processes are evaluated and improved.

7.4   Customer Satisfaction Results

Summarize the organization's customer satisfaction and dissatisfaction results using key measures and/or indicators of these results.

7.5   Customer Satisfaction Comparison

Compare the organization's customer satisfaction results with those of competitors.

APPENDIX C

Tools and Resources

MAGAZINES/NEWSLETTERS/ AUDIOTAPES

Fortune Magazine—Monthly magazine focusing on trends in finance, business, customer service and technology. Includes many interviews with some of the biggest names in business. Available on CompuServe. Ph: 800-523-3131

John Naisbitt's *Trend Letter*—Bulletized newsletter reporting "trends transforming the economy, technology, society and the world." Bimonthly. Ph: 800-368-0115; Fax: 202-333-5198

Executive Book Summaries—Soundview's Executive Book Summaries makes reading books easy by summarizing the latest business books in a 6–8 page summary. They take out all the fluff and filler, leaving facts, data and critical information. Each month are several book summaries. Ph: 800-521-1227

Navigator Newsletter—Quarterly newsletter published by Chart Your Course International. Topic areas include, creating productive work environments,

innovation, teamwork, TQM, human resource management and topics on leader development. Ph: 800-821-2487; Fax: 770-760-0581; E-mail:74344.135 @compuserve.com

Boardroom Reports—This newsletter is published twice a month. Packed with information on management, finances, tax information, healthcare issues, business and lots of other information. Ph: 800-234-3834

Quality Connection—Comes out quarterly and provides information dealing with TQM/CQI in the healthcare industry. Ph: 617-424-4800

Quality Digest—Monthly magazine features easy-read stories about quality award winners, ISO 9000, and business columns from Stephen Covey, Karl Albrecht, Ken Blanchard and Amy Zuckerman. Ph: 916-527-8875; Fax: 916-5276983; E-mail:Qualitydig@ qof.com

Issues & Observations—The Center for Creative Leadership publishes this newsletter several times a year. Topics include, leadership, managing change and management research. Ph: 910-288-7210

Harvard Business Review—Monthly magazine addressing latest developments, case studies and issues in the working world today. Ph: 800-274-3214

Audio-Tech Business Book Summaries—This company narrates the latest business books on audio tape so you can turn your commute to and from work into an educational experience. They do 35 audio summaries a year. Ph: 800-776-1910

The Public Innovator—Published twice monthly by the National Academy of Public Administration Foundation's Alliance for Redesigning Government. They deal with many issues primarily surrounding federal, state and local governments. Ph: 202-466-6887; Fax: 202-347-3252; E-mail:ncjohnson @aol.com

Human Resource Executive—An upbeat monthly magazine focusing on human resource topics. Provides key information, statistics and trends in the HR field. Ph: 215-784-0910 ext. 318

Training Magazine—This magazine is published by Lakewood Publications. Many topics surround training and development. Ph: 800-328-4329; Fax: 612-333-6526; E-Mail:74143.3000 @compuserve.com

AWARDS AND RECOGNITION SPECIALISTS

Medallic Art Company—They manufacture a variety of artistic and presentation quality medals, commemorative plaques, coins, belt buckles, and key chains. Have produced the Pulitzer Prize, Congressional Medal of Honor, the National Medal of Science and others. Ph: 800-843-9854; Fax: 605-332-3175

Creative Awards—Has a extensive catalog containing a vast selection of jewelry, promotional items, glassware, silver, trophies and plaques. The have an "Idea Center" that custom designs special awards based on individual or organizational needs. Ph: 708-593-7700 or 800-492-3439; Fax: 708-593-1155

Award Crafters, Inc.—One of the leaders in innovation, quality, and craftsmanship of achievement and recognition products. Their products include detailed porcelain eagles, fine imported crystal to plaques and architectural tablets. Ph: 703-818-0500; Fax: 301-460-9575

TRAINING FILMS AND VIDEOS

CRM Films
Ph: 800-421-0833
619-931-5792

Excellence in Training Corporation
Ph: 800-747-6569
Fax: 515-276-9476

American Media Incorporated
Ph: 800-262-2557
Fax: 515-224-0256

Films Incorporated
Ph: 800-4222, ext. 44
Fax: 312-878-0416

The Training Edge, Inc.
Ph: 800-292-4375
Fax: 707-776-7031

TRAINING AND EDUCATION SPECIALISTS

The Juran Institute—The Juran Institute was founded by J.M. Juran and is based in Wilton, Connecticut. The Juran Institute is a worldwide leader in research, consulting and training in managing quality. They help organizations apply quality management practices to improve customer loyalty, increase productivity and achieve competitive distinction. Ph: 800-338-7726; Fax: 203-834-9891; Internet: http://www. juran.com

GOAL/QPC—A nonprofit organization designed to promote increased organizational effectiveness and competitiveness thought the use of Total Quality Management and other transformational strategies. GOAL/QPC also offers books, training programs and software. Ph: 800-643-4316; Fax: 508-685-6151

Chart Your Course International—A management consulting firm that helps businesses and people reach their potential and become more productive and profitable. Shows people how to create dynamic, innovative and quality oriented work environments through consulting, training and professional speaking. Ph: 800-821-2487; Fax: 770-760-0581; E-mail: 74344.135 @compuserve.com

BUSINESS RESOURCES/TRAINING PRODUCTS

Crisp Publications—Provides a comprehensive selection of videos, books and workbooks including topics covering management, customer service, retirement, life planning and everything between. Ph: 800-442-7477; Fax: 415-323-5800

Resources for Organizations, Inc.—Bob Pike of the Creative Training Techniques Company, offers fun, stimulating and creative resource materials for trainers. Ph: 800-383-9210; Fax: 612-829-0260

Harvard Business School Press—Backed with the prestigious reputation of the Harvard Business School, they publish an excellent catalog of management books and special reports. Ph: 800-545-7685; Fax: 617-495-6985; Internet: http://bisonnet

Quality Resources—Provides a catalog of practical and authoritative books on quality improvement. Ph: 800-247-8519; Fax: 914-761-9467

Pfeiffer & Company—Provides books, tools, games, activities and references for trainers, consultants and managers. Ph: 800-274-4434; Fax: 800-569-0443

Productivity Press—Offers an extensive catalog of tools and serious books on leadership, management; product design and development, performance measurement, process improvement and customer sales and service. They provide an excellent selection of books published by Japanese management experts. Ph: 800-394-6286; Fax: 800-394-6286

Lakewood Publications—A multipronged organization that helps people and organizations gain better performance and productivity. Their focus is the human side of business. They publish the *Training* magazine monthly. Lakewood also publishes *Potentials in Marketing, Presentations* Magazine, business books and newsletters. They sponsor a Training Conference & Expo each year. Ph: 800-328-4329; Fax: 612-333-6526; E-Mail: 74143.3000@compuserve.com.

Vision Works—A Minneapolis-based company offering visualization tools for innovative thinking. The firm has a rapidly growing customer base, including teams, facilitators, trainers, consultants, managers and executives working in some of the world's largest and most innovative organizations. Order VIS-IT™ Notes by calling (612) 926-7991 or faxing (612) 926-7690 or write to Vision Works at 4845 York Ave. South, Minneapolis, MN 55410.

ON-LINE SERVICES

America Online—AOL's list of services is extensive. You will find several electronic magazines and newspapers like *PC WORLD* and *USA Today.* CNN Online is represented as well. StockLink, news and finance, business news, sports and classifieds help you make decisions and keep you informed from the convenience of your home. AOL also serves as a gateway to the Internet and comes with a WWW browser. Ph: 800-827-6364, 703-448-8700; WWW:www.aol.com

CompuServe—CIS is similar to AOL but the setup is slightly different. The Standard Pricing Plan includes news, sports and weather, a reference library, shopping, money, stocks & finance, member support services, games & entertainment, travel & leisure and many more. The forums, for which you pay connect charges, range from education to foreign language, religion, space, working-from-home, show-biz to almost any issue discussion you can think of. Provides WWW access through a NetLauncher browser. Ph: 800-848-8199, 614-457-0802

Microsoft Network—Provides similar services as listed in the other on-line services. Provides the Internet Explorer for Windows 95 users. Ph: 800-386-5550; WWW: http://www.msn.com

Prodigy—Has an interface that is very colorful and there is even some animation. The company provides an electronic bulletin board helping college seniors find potential job leads. Counselors also provide helpful information on writing resumes and interview preparation. High school seniors have direct access to academic information and admissions procedures to college and universities around the United States. Ph: 800-776-3449; WWW: http://www.prodigy.com

ASSOCIATIONS, NETWORKS AND ALLIANCES

Society of Human Resource Managers (SHRM)—70,000 member organization represents the human resource profession. Provides its members with education and information services, conferences and seminars, government and media representation, and publications that equip human resource professionals for their roles as leaders and decision makers within their organizations. Ph: 800-2837476; Fax: 703-836-0367

American Society of Training and Administration (ASTD)—This professional organization represents people in the training and consulting industry. They provide full range of services including publications, conferences and advice and assistance. Local chapters in major cities across the country. Ph: 703-683-8100; Fax: 703-683-8103

National Performance Review (NPR)—The organization designed to help reinvent the federal government. Published numerous products and reports including, *From Red Tape to Results: Creating a Government That Works Better and Costs Less.* Ph: 202-632-0150; Fax: 202-632-0390; E-mail:rego.news @npr.gsa.gov. They have a web page where you can download information, reports, newsletters and speeches. Internet address: http://www.npr.gov

The American Society for Quality Control (ASQC)—One of the nation's largest quality management organizations. Local chapters across the country; focus on both the technical and people side of quality improvement and quality control; publishes *Quality Progress* and *The Public Sector Network,* which primarily deals with the government industry. Ph: 414-272-8575 or 800-248-1946

The New Leader
Registration Form

DO YOU HAVE A SUCCESS STORY?

We are looking for examples of excellence in action. We invite you to become a contributor to one of our future books and newsletters. If you have a story about excellent customer service, leadership, innovation or just a new way of doing something, please let us know!

Mail, E-mail or fax to:
Chart Your Course International
2814 Highway 212, SW
Conyers, GA 30208
Phone: 1-800-821-2487
Fax: 770-760-0581
E-mail:
74344.135@compuserve.com

My Story:

(use back if needed)

❑ *May we use your story in our newsletter and publications?*

❑ *Would you like to receive a complimentary six-month subscription to our newsletter?*

❑ *May we call you for more information on your story?*

Your name_____

Title:_____

Organization:_____# of employees_____

Daytime address:_____

City:_____

State/Prov._____Zip/Postal Code:_____Country_____

Daytime phone_____Fax#_____

E-mail:_____

BIBLIOGRAPHY

"A Portrait of America." Special Supplement to *Business Week/Reinventing America*, 1992, p. 511.

"An Incentive to Work." Editorial in *The Atlanta Journal-Constitution*, September 21, 1995, p. A16.

"Ann Landers." *Atlanta Journal-Constitution*, July 23, 1995, p. M7.

Associated Press. "Paperwork Driving Up Health-care Expenses." *The San Antonio Express-News*, January 19, 1993, p. 1-C.

———. "Office Pool Claims 20% of Lotto Prize." *The San Antonio Express-News*, March 18, 1994, p. 17A.

Bagin, Don. "Let's Stop Wasteful Meetings," *Communication Briefings*.

Ballard, Robert D. *Exploring the Titantic*. Ontario: Madison Press Books, 1988.

Barker, Joel A. *Paradigms*, New York: Harper Collins, 1992.

Barry, Dave. "The 90s. Looking Back at the Interactive Salad Bar." *Newsweek*, January 3, 1994, p. 53.

Bay, Austin. "High-tech Takes to Battlefield." *The San Antonio Express News*, May 26, 1994, p. 6D.

Bednarek, David I. "Go, Team, Go." *Human Resource Executive*, April 1994, pp. 42–45.

Bender, Steve. "They Teach Our Children Well." *Southern Living*, June 1990.

Boroughs, Don L. "Bureaucracy Busters." *U.S. News and World Report*, November 30, 1992, pp. 49–54.

Business Week. 1992 special supplement *Reinventing America*.

247

Cauley, Leslie. *USA Today,* August 23, 1993.

Christensen, Mike. "In Government We Distrust." *Atlanta-Journal Constitution,* April 30, 1995, p. A8.

Coyle, Wanda, "Customer Service Gets Attention for De Mar." *The Fresno Bee,* December 24, 1991.

Crichton, Michael. *Jurassic Park.* New York: Ballantine Books, 1992.

Crozier, Michel. *The Bureaucratic Phenomenon.* Chicago: The University of Chicago Press, 1964.

Deming, W. Edwards. *Out of the Crisis.* Cambridge, MA: MIT-CAES, 1986, pp. 3-58, 248.

Dow Jones Service. "Frustrated PC Users Flood Help Lines." *The San Antonio Express-News,* March 4, 1994. p. 8E.

Downs, Anthony. *Inside Bureaucracy.* Boston: Little, Brown and Company, 1967.

Drucker, Peter F. *Innovation and Entrepreneurship.* New York: Harper & Row, 1994.

Dumaine, Brian. "The Trouble With Teams." *Fortune,* September 5, 1994, p. 86-92.

———. "The Bureaucracy Busters." *Fortune,* June 17, 1991, p. 37.

———. "Who Needs A Boss?" *Fortune,* May 7, 1990, p. 53.

Finley, Don. "Medical Network Planned." *The San Antonio Express News,* December 8, 1993.

Fisher, Ann B. "Morale Crisis." *Fortune,* November 1991, p. 71.

———. "CEO's Think That Morale is Dandy." *Fortune,* November 18, 1991, p. 83.

Flower, Joe. "The Role of the Leader. *Healthcare Forum Journal,* May-June 1990, p. 32

Friedman, Milton. "Gammon's Law Points to Health-Care Solution." *The Wall Street Journal,* November 12, 1991.

Friedman, Dana E. "Child Care for Employees' Kids." *Harvard Business Review,* March-April, 1986, pp. 28–32.

Gammon, Max. "The Growth of bur in the British National Health Service." *The Journal of Management in Medicine* 3 (Oct 1988).

Gourley, Scott. "Long-Distance Operators." *Popular Mechanics*, September 1995, pp. 64–67.

Government Executive. Al Gore quoted in September 1993, p. 7.

Harris Poll as reported by Grant Ujifusa.

Helm, Leslie. "High-Tech House Calls Catching On." *Los Angeles Times*, April 28, 1994, p. A19.

———. "Patience Till the Promise Pays Off." Special edition of *Business Week /Innovation* ,1989.

Henkoff, Ronald. "Make Your Office More Productive." *Fortune*, February 25, 1991, pp. 72–84.

Henry, Jane, and David Walker. *Managing Innovation.* Beverly Hills, CA: Sage Publications, 1991.

Iaccoca, Lee. Career Track Audio tape.

Jaffe, Charles A. "Moving Fast Standing Still." *Nation's Business*, October 1991, pp. 57–59.

Japan Human Relations Association. *The Idea Book*, Cambridge, MA: Productivity Press, 1988.

Jaques, Elliott. "In Praise of Hierarchy." *Harvard Business Review*, January-February 1990.

Kanter, Rosabeth M. "Quality Leadership and Change." *Quality Progress*, February 1987.

Katzenbach, Jon R., and Douglas K. Smith. *The Wisdom of Teams.* McKinsey & Company, Inc., 1993.

Landes, Les. "Leading the Duck at Mission Control." *Quality Progress* ,July 1995, pp. 43–48.

Levering, Robert. "A Great Place to Work." *Soundview Executive Book Summaries*, 11 (July 1989), pp. 2–8.

Look Outs, 10 (January 1995). The University of Georgia, Athens, GA.

Loomis, Carol J. "Dinosaurs?" *Fortune*, May 3, 1993, pp. 36–42.

Lutz, Sandy. "Hospitals Stretch Their Creativity to Motivate Workers." *Modern Heathcare*, March 5, 1990, p. 20.

Moawab, Bob. Speech made in San Antonio, TX, 1994.

Mackenzie, Alec. *The Time Trap*. New York: AMACOM, 1990, p. 136.

McKenna, Joseph. "Empowerment Thins a Forest of Bureaucracy." *Industry Week*, April 5, 1992, p. 64.

"Medicine: Cost of Technology Has Dropped." *Los Angeles Times*, April 28, 1994.

Mercury, August 1995, p. 1. The Army Medical Department, San Antonio, TX.

Miller, Celome. Phone conversation, VA Medical Center, Portland, OR.

Morgan and Banks Report, cited in *Knightview*. Christchurch, New Zealand: Knight Consulting Group Ltd.

Naj Kumar, Amal. "Not-Nearby Doctor Helps Agile Robot Perform Surgery." *The Wall Street Journal*, March 4, 1994, p. B6.

New York Times, May 1,1983, p. F-3.

Paulson, Terry L. *They Shoot Managers Don't They?* Berkeley, CA: Ten Speed Press, 1991.

Pearson, Andral E. "Tough-Minded Ways to Get Innovative." Special issue on Innovation, *Harvard Business Review*, 1991.

Peters, Tom. *On Achieving Excellence Newsletter*. Pala Alto, CA: Tom Peters Group/Communications, 1993.

———. *On Achieving Excellence Newsletter*, Vol. 7, No. 3, Mar 1992, p. 2.

Quinn, Matthew C. "Facing Economic Challenges." *The Atlanta Journal-Constitution*, March 30, 1995, p. E1.

Rehfeld, John. "What Working for a Japanese Company Taught Me." *Harvard Business Review*, November-December 1990. p. 167.

Reich, Robert. "Hire Education." *Rolling Stone*, October 20, 1994, p. 119.

Reid, Peter. *Well Made in America*. New York: McGraw-Hill, 1990.

Ribaric, Ronald F. "Mission Impossible: Meeting Family Demands." *Personnel Administrator*, August 1987, pp. 70–78.

Ritz-Carlton Quality Day Orientation, Atlanta, GA, June 1995.

Schaffer, Robert. "How to Tap the Zest Factor." *The New York Times*, 1989.

Scholtes, Peter R. *The TEAM Handbook*. Madison, WI: Joiner and Associates, 1988, pp. 2-8.

Shultze, Horst. Speech made to ASTD National Conference, Atlanta, GA, June 1992.

Speech delivered to Alamo Federal Executive Board, San Antonio, TX, July 1993.

Greenburg, Rueben. Speech presented in San Antonio, TX, July 1995.

Stayer, Ralph. "How I Learned to Let My Workers Lead." *Harvard Business Review*, November-December, 1990.

Survey reported in *Human Resource Executive*, Dec 1993, p. 40.

Symonds, William. "Getting Rid of Paper is Just the Beginning." *Business Week*, December 21, 1992, p. 88.

Tarkenton, Fran, and Tad Tuleaja. *How to Motivate People*. New York: Harper & Row, 1986.

"The New Business Game by Peter Drucker." *Bottom Line Personal*, March 30, 1993.

Thompson, Victor. *Bureaucracy and Innovation*. University of Alabama Press, 1969.

Thurston, Scott. "Southwest's Wacky, Low-cost World." *The Atlanta Journal-Constitution*, July 17, 1994, p. C1.

Total Employee Involvement. PRODUCTIVITY, Inc., 3 (March 1990).

Tschohl, John. *Short Term Victories: Successful Strategies for coping with the Total Quality Time Lag*. Minneapolis, MN: Advanced Management Group, 1993.

Walton, Mary. *The Deming Management Method*. New York: Putnam Publishing Group, 1986.

Wayne, Windy, and Sandra Burud. "A Hospital's On-Site Child Care Center Proves to Make Business Sense." *HCM Review*, Summer 1986, pp. 81–85.

Wheatley, Margaret J. *Leadership and the New Science*. San Francisco: Berrett-Koehler Publishers, 1992.

WordPerfect Report. Spring 1994, VIII (1), p. 4.

Workforce 2000. Redwood City, CA: ADIA & Towers Perrin.

INDEX